BEINHORN'S

MESQUITE
COOKERY

BEINHORN'S
MESQUITE
COOKERY

BY COURTENAY BEINHORN
With Wine Suggestions by
Gerald Asher, Wine Editor
of *Gourmet* Magazine.

★

Texas Monthly Press

Texas Monthly Press, Inc.
P.O. Box 1569
Austin, Texas 78767

A B C D E F G H

Library of Congress Cataloging-in-Publication Data

Beinhorn, Courtenay, 1948–
  Beinhorn's mesquite cookery.

  1. Barbecue cookery. 2. Mesquite. I. Asher,
Gerald. II. Title. III. Title: Mesquite cookery.
TX840.B3B434 1986   641.5′784   86-6009
ISBN 0-87719-060-7

Book design by HIXO, Inc.
Illustrations copyright © 1986 by HIXO, Inc.
Cover photograph by Robert Latorre
Copyright © 1986 Robert Latorre Productions Inc.
Food styled by Gourmet Express, Dallas, Texas.

For Big Bee and Alexandra

Contents

PREFACE

Cooking with mesquite is such a natural part of culinary life in the Southwest that until recently, no one gave it a second thought. For hundreds of years, Comanches and chuckwagon chefs alike prized its fiery, long-lasting coals and the distinctively sweet, smoky aroma that underscored the good flavor of all manner of foods, from native quail and venison to beef steaks and sourdough bread cooked up in a Dutch oven. But for all its culinary assets, mesquite remained a purely regional passion.

That is, until the rise of the "new American cuisine." Whispers about a remarkable grilling fuel first surfaced on the West Coast. At restaurants like Berkeley's famed Chez Panisse, chefs Alice Waters and Jeremiah Tower were using mesquite charcoal to bring out the naturally good flavor of delicacies such as spring lamb with fresh herbs and rockfish served with a tomato-onion relish.

The whispers grew louder in New York, when cookbook author and chef John Clancy began to grill seafood over mesquite in his Greenwich Village restaurant. Soon, orders for the wood-grilled fish outnumbered other dishes two to one. The favorite of Clancy's patrons was skewered swordfish, marinated in lemon juice and grated onion, cooked over mesquite with fragrant Turkish bay leaves.

By then, the word was out about an exotic wood— no one could pronounce its name—that imparted an extraordinary taste to grilled food. For a time, Clancy was one of the few New York chefs with a steady supply of the wood. Friends in Texas shipped it to him at freight charges so high he might well have bought a bus ticket for each sack.

Now when you have a near-exclusive on a hot property like mesquite, you do your best to keep your source a well guarded secret. So Clancy quite naturally ignored rival chefs when they begged for the name of his supplier. Rumor had it that at least one rival, goaded to a frenzy of jealousy, sent spies to sniff out the shipper's name.

What happened next was inevitable, but in a very small way I suppose I'm partly to blame. I managed to wangle an article assignment from Alex Ward, then editor of *The New York Times*' "Living" section, by convincing him that, as a native Texan whose family ranch was covered with the stuff, I knew more about mesquite than any other living soul in New York. The article, which appeared on June 23, 1982, was called "Mesquite: Bad Press but Great Flavor." It included the remarks of a few restaurant chefs who were using the wood, but the clincher came at the end where I listed two mail order sources for mesquite wood and charcoal.

The morning the article appeared, it seems that pandemonium broke loose. Telephone lines into both suppliers were jammed as eager chefs rushed to place their orders. Within days calls were pouring in from Washington, Boston, Minneapolis, and a dozen other cities. By the end of the month, one purveyor of the wood had orders totaling $75,000 and was selling the wood to outlanders at the outrageous (for Texas) price of $1 a pound.

The rest is history, of course. As our love affair with regional tastes intensified, the mesquite grill became the signature of many restaurants specializing in the new American cuisine. At one point, it seemed as though clouds of flavorful smoke were pouring out of at least half the new eateries on the east and west coasts. On the home front, major charcoal manufacturers added mesquite sawdust to their briquets—admittedly, with less than satisfactory results.

The American public shows no signs of letting up on its passion for good food cooked over mesquite. Time has produced a band of talented chefs who know how to use the fuel to good advantage, and their ranks continue to grow. The numbers tell the story: The Dallas manufacturer of the professional Aztec Mesquite Grill, one of the most popular restaurant grills designed especially for use with the wood, had sales of $800,000 in 1984 and $2 million in 1985. For home chefs, there has been a steadily increasing supply of both mesquite wood and charcoal—much of it available year-round in supermarkets and gourmet stores.

This brings us to the reason for this cookbook. It is time, I think, to put mesquite into a culinary perspective: to clearly explain which flavors it enhances and which it does not, when to use mesquite wood and when the charcoal, and how to add other aromatic flavors to the mesquite grill. Above all, I would like to encourage readers to put aside petroleum-based charcoal briquets and discover the down-to-earth pleasures of cooking with wood and pure charcoal.

The recipes in this book owe much to my own upbringing in San Antonio and points south. If it seems as though there are a great many dishes using chiles, garlic, cumin, cilantro, and other spices of the Mexican kitchen, it is because the flavors are native to the areas in which mesquite is most abundant. As it happens, they have a natural affinity for each other.

In the course of doing research on mesquite (mostly of the eating variety), I found that flavors from other culinary traditions also marry well with its aroma. So you will also find recipes from the Mediterranean, tasting of rosemary, fennel, and olive oil, and from Japan, India, and Southeast Asia, flavored with soy sauce, sesame oil, lemon grass, ginger, cardamom, and other aromatic spices.

What most of the recipes have in common is simplicity. Two-thirds require just 30 minutes or so of actual hands-on preparation before being placed on the grill. Many can be fixed ahead of time and left to marinate in the refrigerator or in a cool kitchen until you are ready to cook. The idea is to keep the preliminaries to a minimum, so that the chef can savor more primal pleasures: the fragrance of burning mesquite wood, the beauty of the flames licking against the evening sky, and above all the delicious flavor of the food cooked over this extraordinary fuel.

Courtenay Beinhorn
New York City

■ *WHERE?*
Mesquite grows in: Texas, New Mexico, Arizona, California, Utah, Colorado, Nevada, Oklahoma, Kansas, Missouri, Louisiana, Hawaii, Mexico, Peru, Argentina, Chile, Jamaica, The Bahamas, The Philippines, India, Pakistan, South Africa, Australia.

MANY THANKS

I am deeply grateful to the following people who helped to make this cookbook happen:

Peter Felker, who invited me to speak on the culinary uses of mesquite at a Los Amigos del Mesquite gathering three years ago. It was at that dinner the idea for this cookbook was born.

Morton MacLeod, who provided good counsel and encouragement throughout this project, along with innumerable bags of his fine mesquite wood.

Weber-Stephen Products Company, for whom I consulted on an outdoor cooking project involving four woods—mesquite, hickory, oak, and alder.

Gerald Asher, who graciously shared his lucid thinking and superior knowledge of wine in the chapter on wines with mesquite-grilled food.

Lindsey Shere, pastry chef at Chez Panisse, who contributed her good ideas on desserts to serve with food cooked over mesquite.

Deborah Black, Victoria Dunk, Aurora Rodriguez, Carmen Ramos, and Lucy Sepulveda, who happily parted with some of their best family recipes.

My parents, William and Phyllis Beinhorn, and my brother, Alston Beinhorn, whose greater knowledge of the brush country and careful reading of this manuscript kept me from tripping over hidden brambles. More than a few recipes in the book are better for my mother's suggestions.

My husband, William Dunk, whose sensitive palate and cast-iron stomach stood him in good stead as chief taster, helpful critic, and creative idea man.

And finally, our baby daughter, Alexandra, who brought us so much joy during the making of this cookbook.

1
INTRODUCTION

A fellow from South Texas once remarked, with the sly grin that precedes the most preposterous lies, "You know, down here in the brush country, nearly everything you see will either stick you or sting you."

In fact, he was not exaggerating. If you doubt the truth of this notion, just head out to the San Ysidro Ranch early some morning before the sun begins its relentless glare. When you pass the Camino Real tank and get to the marker that commemorates the old seventeenth century trade route from Mexico, pull over and park your truck. Then walk a little way into the brush and pace off an area of, say, 100 square feet.

On this tiny patch of Texas, you'll find more sticking, biting, stabbing, scratching creatures than anywhere but the Amazonian jungle. To your left, for instance, are brambly clumps of black brush studded with brittle thorns. Careful now, or you'll step on that pitaya cactus, the one that looks like a cluster of worms, their droopy heads bristling with spines. Just ahead of you, its 100 legs slinking across the earth in perfect synchroneity, is the fierce, red-headed centipede. Don't touch the prickly pear atop the nopal cactus, or your fingers will sting with pain from its hair-like thorns. And as you wisely keep one eye on that nest of angrily buzzing yellow jackets, be sure to keep one eye on the column of great red ants marching across your boot tip.

On this stickery plot of land there is just one friendly being: the mesquite. At first glance this scrubby tree may not seem entirely amiable. Its gnarled trunk and branches are twisted like snakes, its reddish-brown bark is scaly, and under its cloak of feathery green leaves lurk two-inch thorns of such rapier sharpness that they rival the dreaded "cat claw," also known as the "wait-a-minute bush". (Every time you get caught by its thorns, you have to call out "Hey, wait a minute!" while you get unstuck.)

Mesquite's reputation is even worse than its appearance. Cursed as a "scavenger tree," it's been called "noxious," "malignant," "a bitter weed," "the scourge of the Southwest." On an unpopularity scale, it ranks right down there with rattlers,

coyotes, and tumbleweed. But all this mudslinging is not quite fair, for although mesquite has its faults, its forgotten virtues far outweigh its—shall we say—antisocial characteristics.

If the mesquite tree were human, I would imagine it would take the form of a genial outlaw, rather like a scruffy sort of Robin Hood. The tree is certainly a thief, for it has an astonishing thirst. Its water-sucking taproot has been known to plunge 175 feet deep into the earth, while other roots may radiate outward 50 to 60 feet in an unending search for moisture. Once it locates water, the tree greedily drinks every drop from the parched soil, leaving forage grasses to wither in the heat.

At its most rapacious, mesquite can spread faster than a brushfire in August. Between 1850 and 1950, the tree invaded more than 75 million acres of rangeland across the Southwest. Today it infests 55 million acres in Texas alone. How it rose up from its native habitat of arroyos, riverbanks, and wet bottomlands to conquer the lush grasslands is a sad tale of land mismanagement. Overgrazing and brushfires deliberately set to clear the land, complicated by drought and floods, all prepared the way for mesquite's onslaught.

It is also the story of the great cattle drives of the nineteenth century, when men like Charles Goodnight and Oliver Loving drove their herds of longhorns thousands of dusty miles through West Texas and New Mexico to markets in Colorado and Kansas. Along the way hungry cattle and horses chomped on sweet-tasting mesquite beans. The indigestible seeds passed through the livestock, and wherever they were "planted," new seedlings sprang up. For years cattle trails everywhere were dotted with clumps of mesquite.

Lately, this explanation for the tree's proliferation has fallen into disrepute, but it is true that once mesquite has put down roots, it is almost impossible to get rid of. Unchecked, it will grow into impenetrable thickets, so dense that cattle can stay hidden in them for years. For half a century ranchers have tried to halt mesquite's relentless encroachment in a dozen different ways. Bulldozing or chopping the tree above ground only stimulates the root system to send up new shoots. Root

A MESQUITE IS A MESQUITE IS A . . .
What's in a name? All mesquite trees belong to the genus Prosopis, *the old Greek word for burdock. In California, the* Prosopis glandulosa *var.* torreyana *is better known as the western honey mesquite. In Arizona, there's* Prosopis velutina, *or velvet mesquite. And in Texas, there are millions of acres of* Prosopis glandulosa *var.* glandulosa, *a.k.a. the plain old honey mesquite.*

The word "mesquite" may be a derivative of the ancient Aztec name for the tree—mizquitl. In Hawaii, mesquite is known as kiawe. Other aliases include the western honey locust, the honeypod, and the Texas ironwood.

4

plowing is more effective, but expensive. Only poison will actually destroy the tree—until seeds scattered by livestock and wild game produce a fresh crop of mesquite.

All these peccadillos would certainly add up to an unsavory character were it not for mesquite's all but forgotten generosity to the Indians, explorers, and pioneers who settled the Southwest. What the tree takes with one hand, it gives back lavishly and unstintingly with the other—but only to those who know how to use its extraordinary gifts.

The slender yellow pods or beans that dangle from mesquite's green-shaded boughs in summer—the same that fueled the tree's invasion of the range—once were a vital source of wild food. In 1528 the Spanish explorer Alvar Núñez Cabeza DeVaca reached Texas and spent six years among the Indians. His travel account, *La Relación,* included what is probably the first written mention of mesquite, as he recorded how one tribe pounded the pods into meal and then mixed it with earth and water. "This mesquiqez," he wrote, "is a fruit which, while on the tree, is very bitter and like the carob bean. It is eaten with earth and then becomes sweet and very palatable."

Hundreds of years later, travelers in the Southwest found that mesquite flour was a dietary staple for many Indian tribes. In 1854, James G. Bell, a cattleman on his way to California with a herd of Texas steers, observed the Pima Indians grinding the pods in an earthen mortar with a wooden pestle. To this flour they added water, and when it was ready, they shaped the wet meal into loaves and let it harden. The remaining "liquor" was drunk. Of the bread, Bell wrote, "It has a honey sweet taste and would be palatable but for their dirty manner of making it."

Time and time again, mesquite beans saved the lives of famished surveyors and traders trekking across unknown territory. J. Frank Dobie tells of a Texas ranger who ran across a group of Mexican "freighters" out in the brush. Waylaid by Indians and stripped of their supplies, the ragtag bunch had managed to survive by eating rattlesnakes, prickly pears, and

mesquite beans. When the ranger asked how they could live on such fare, he received this answer: "Con tunas solo se puede vivir, pero con tunas y mesquite los dos se engorda mucho." ("With prickly pears alone one can live, but with prickly pears and mesquite beans, a person will get fat.")

In fact, mesquite beans are quite nutritious. The fiber of the pods contains 13% protein and as much as 36% grape sugar, which makes them palatable to man and positively delectable to livestock. Bulls have been known to batter whole limbs off the trunk of a mesquite tree to get at the beans, while goats will clamber right up into the branches to nibble at the fruit. During the Indian wars in New Mexico, the U.S. Cavalry paid 3¢ a pound for the pods to use as horse feed. By 1897, mesquite beans were fetching $1 a bushel in San Antonio.

What is miraculous about the pods is that they are most abundant when they are most needed—in times of drought. In *The Coming Empire* (1877), H. F. McDaniel and N. A. Taylor described this phenomenon, which holds true today: "When the rains have been abundant and the grasses unusually luxuriant, the mesquite yields but a slim crop of beans; when the rains have been moderate, and the grasses are of moderate luxuriance, the crop is greatly increased; but when the drought has been severe and the grass is poor, the mesquite is literally burdened with its clusters of rich pods."

Such generosity almost makes up for mesquite's bad habits, but every other part of the tree also yields extraordinary gifts. In spring the lacy green leaves give a lush look to the brush country, but provide so little shade from summer's merciless sun that one early traveler wrote, "To find shade under a mesquite tree is like dipping water with a sieve." The Indians knew, though, that the leaves could produce magical elixirs that would cure a dozen ailments.

Centuries ago, the ancient Aztecs discovered that "mizquitl" leaves, ground up and mixed with water, made a soothing lotion for sore eyes. Later, tribes such as the Apaches, Pimas, and Maricopas, who suffered from eye inflammations common to those who lived in smoke-filled dwellings, used infu-

DESIGNER BEANS
Mesquite pods or beans come in all shapes and sizes. Some look like elongated string beans; some are curved like crescent moons; others are as curly as a piglet's tail.

Whatever their guise, all mesquite beans are rich in sugar and protein. In times past, they've been converted into everything from cups of flour to cups of coffee.

6

sions of the leaves or the sap to relieve the irritation. The Comanches chewed the bitter leaves to ease toothaches, while the Yumas brewed a tea to treat venereal infections. For headaches, the Yaqui Indians beat the leaves to a pulp, added urine, and applied the mixture to the forehead. And if that weren't enough, frontier women discovered that a handful of mesquite leaves tossed into a cast-iron washpot would brighten their laundry.

Both Indians and settlers made a tea from the white inner bark, which is high in tannin, to cure diarrhea. One tribe used the bark to relieve indigestion; another used it to curdle milk. Others pounded the bark until it was soft and pliable enough to use for baby diapers. The tough, gnarled root, boiled in water, made a salve for flesh wounds, as well as a tonic for colic and nervousness. Pioneer children fashioned toothbrushes, whips, and quirts from the roots; their mothers used the hard thorns as pins—a practice still followed by cowboys today.

Even the golden drops of gum that ooze from the bark of some trees were prized by the Indians. It could mend broken pottery and turn gray hair black again. White men began to collect the gum in the 1870s, hoping that it might replace gum arabic. In 1872, 24,000 pounds were gathered in Texas and used to prepare gum drops, mucilage, and jujube paste, but the expected boom never materialized.

No part of the tree was more useful to the first Southwestern settlers than the wood. The switch mesquite that has overrun so much of the range is too small and twisted to provide good lumber, but the trees did provide wood for livestock pens and small cabins. The posts of the first barbed wire fences were made of the wood. Large mesquite trees produced the original timbers of the Alamo and the Tumacacori Mission in Arizona. In the 1880s, the streets of San Antonio were paved with hexagonal blocks of mesquite wood, and as late as the 1940s, one observer wrote that "the best streets" in Buenos Aires were still paved with the wood.

Today, all of mesquite's sterling virtues have been forgotten. Folk remedies have given way to aspirin and antacids, only

cattle and wild game graze on the pods, and the tree is widely excoriated as a weed. So much abuse has been heaped upon the poor mesquite that it may be the only tree to have a band of supporters—Los Amigos del Mesquite—dedicated to changing its unsavory image.

And, unlike the Flat Earth Society, the group has achieved a measure of success. Little by little, the public is learning that mesquite need not be a pest. Its very presence can be viewed as part of nature's healing process, as the tree returns vast quantities of nitrogen to soil starved by overgrazing and drought. On a controlled basis, native grasses will flourish alongside the mesquite. Along with other brush, the tree provides cover for white-tailed deer, quail, dove, and other game. And in semiarid regions, such as Argentina and the Sudan, mesquite serves as a barrier between desert and farmland.

Donald Peattie said it best in his *Natural History of Western Trees:* "Mesquite is something more than a tree; it is almost an elemental force, comparable to fire—too valuable to extinguish completely and too dangerous to trust unwatched."

■ *TREE FRIENDS*
Is mesquite just a pain in the neck? Hell, no, say Los Amigos del Mesquite. Founded in 1984, this non-for-profit organization is made up of 126 of the tree's most ardent supporters. Four times a year, Los Amigos publish a chatty and opinionated newsletter. Recent issues have included articles on using mesquite as a landscape ornamental, making mesquite furniture and jewelry, and milling mesquite flour.

Every fall, the group holds a fun weekend convention in Texas—2 days of scholarly presentations, wood-working demonstrations, and more. For information write: P.O. Box 15551, Northeast Station, Austin, TX 78761.

Years ago J. Frank Dobie, a keen observer of life in the brush country, wrote at length about mesquite and the pleasures of its distinctive aroma. He recalled a friend who always held his hands in the smoke of the breakfast fire so that they would smell of the burning wood the rest of the morning. As for himself, Dobie opined, "Smelling a mesquite fire on a cool morning and drinking coffee boiled over it can never be forgotten by anyone with strong senses," and he praised the flavor mesquite gives to a steak cooked over its fiery coals.

As Southwesterners have long known, the delectable fragrance of the wood is reason enough to stock the larder with sacks of mesquite. Once you have watched the flames lick over a blazing log, listened to the wood sing and pop, and savored the tantalizing aroma of, say, a brace of juicy little quail basted in tequila as they sizzle over a bed of glowing coals, it is hard to think of ever using chemically laced briquets with their attendant odors of petroleum and lighter fluid.

On a purely practical level, mesquite is a superb cooking fuel. Its dense, hard wood produces a hotter fire and longer-lasting coals than virtually any other wood or charcoal. Indeed, in 1984 *Sunset Magazine* ran tests showing that mesquite charcoal burned at an average maximum temperature of 500°F, while briquets burned at a cooler 460°F. An hour later, the mesquite coals were producing heat of 350°F, while the briquets had fallen to 250°F—scarcely enough heat to cook a piece of squash, much less a thick steak.

Mesquite's hotter fire sears food quickly, sealing in juices and natural flavor. Once you're accustomed to cooking with the wood or charcoal, you'll find that you can use slightly less fuel than you would briquets. When the coals are laid in a single, compact layer, they produce a strong, long-lasting heat that cooks food more quickly and evenly. You can even save unused coals for another day if you cover the grill and close the vents after you've finished cooking.

Ranchers and other people who have mesquite growing outside the back door are well versed in the ways of mixing dry, seasoned logs with green twigs for a wonderfully fragrant fire.

HOW TO COOK WITH MESQUITE WOOD AND CHARCOAL

The rest of us, however, must cook with mesquite sold in three forms: wood chunks, wood chips, and pure hardwood charcoal. Here are some tips on the best way to use each of them.

Wood chunks are sold in sacks that contain fist-sized pieces of wood mixed with smaller chunks and bits of kindling. Most of this wood is harvested from ranchland in Texas and Arizona and is chunked by Rube Goldberg–like machines that cut tree limbs into more or less uniform pieces. The finest mesquite chunks, such as those sold by Bloomfield Farms in Los Altos, California, are free of chemicals and have been heat-treated to kill off the insect population and to reduce the moisture content so that the chunks light easily.

Wood chunks may serve either as a primary fuel or to add extra flavor to a charcoal fire. At first, cooking over a wood-chunk fire may seem a little tricky, since the smaller pieces tend to burn up more quickly than ordinary charcoal. However, the splendid aroma makes the effort more than worthwhile, and with a little practice you'll find that you develop a feel for this method of grilling.

As a rule, 12 to 14 large chunks mixed with the smaller pieces and a little kindling will produce enough coals to cook 2 good-sized steaks or a couple of trout. By adding more wood to the fire, you can build up a strong bed of coals that will last 45 minutes or so—just enough time to cook a slab of baby back ribs or a chicken split in half.

A mesquite wood fire produces the most intense aroma and is best used with stronger tasting foods such as pork, wild game, and leeks, which can stand up to its assertive flavor. Mesquite and beef seem to have a natural affinity for each other, and it also marries well with foods that have been aggressively seasoned with hot chile peppers, lime, cumin, soy sauce, and the like.

The flip side of the coin is that the aroma of a mesquite wood fire may overpower more delicately flavored seafood, or certain meats such as lamb. Here, you can "tame" mesquite's assertive presence by mixing it with pure hardwood charcoal. A few chunks will add a whiff of mesquite aroma to whatever

■ *TOUGH STUFF*
Mesquite wood is twice as hard as hickory or white oak. Its density (.70) is higher than African ebony or sugar maple. It can withstand onslaughts of heat and cold, wind and rain— which is why there are still 100-year-old mesquite fence posts standing in South Texas today.

is on the grill, while combining equal quantities of the wood and charcoal will produce a rich, full-bodied, mellow flavor. You can also create other pleasing fragrances by mixing mesquite chunks with woods such as oak or apple.

Occasionally you may run across a bag of wood chunks that burn with a harsh, acrid smoke. This is unfortunate, but also inevitable: There are at least 44 varieties of mesquite, and it is almost impossible to tell which trees are sweet and which are bitter in flavor. Indeed, there is an old Texas border saying that "Bitter mesquite and poor men's children are common." Some Texans, on the other hand, like to say that all the bitter mesquite comes from Arizona—a claim that is not quite true.

Wood chips are usually the by-products of mesquite chunking operations and are used to add a smoky mesquite flavor to a plain charcoal fire. To do this, you soak the chips in water for 30 minutes or so and then spread them evenly on the hot coals. Within a minute or two, they will begin to smoke furiously. Wood chips produce the most pleasing aroma when they are combined with mesquite or any other hardwood charcoal. Although some producers claim that they will also add mesquite flavor to food cooked on gas or electric grills, I have rarely found this to be true.

By using wood chips, you can more easily control the amount of flavor the food absorbs while cooking. Indeed, you might think of chips as a kind of seasoning, not unlike salt or strong spices such as clove or nutmeg. The intensity of the mesquite fragrance will depend entirely on the quantity of chips that are tossed onto the coals. A small handful will add a bit of flavor, while several cupfuls will produce a pronounced mesquite taste.

It is good to remember, however, that wet chips will produce a distinctly smoky taste—as opposed to the mellower, more full-bodied aroma of a pure wood fire. As a result, I prefer to use wet chips when cooking foods that are enhanced by a very strong, smoky flavor such as barbecued pork for tacos or venison chili. They are also a great way to add mesquite flavor to foods that must be cooked for a long

time, such as wild turkey or beef brisket.

This brings us to *mesquite charcoal,* considered by many professional grill chefs to be the finest fuel available today. Most pure mesquite charcoal comes from Sonora in northern Mexico, where the wood is abundant, labor is cheap, and the Environmental Protection Agency has no jurisdiction. Mesquite logs are stacked, Yaqui Indian style, in a pyramid on top of the ground or in a pit dug into the earth. The logs are covered with straw, burlap, and dirt and are then set alight. The fire will smolder inside for 2 to 3 weeks as the wood is slowly converted into chunks of irregularly shaped charcoal.

The result is a superb cooking fuel that burns very hot, sealing in both juices and flavor. What it will not do, however, is add more than a hint of mesquite aroma to the food that is being cooked. Although the pure charcoal will burn with a pleasing fragrance, most of the flavor will have dissipated by the time the coals are ready. Any residual aroma will be extremely mild.

The very lack of flavor makes mesquite charcoal a fine, all-purpose fuel, ideal for cooking delicately flavored fish or meats such as lamb, which tend to be overpowered by the aroma of a wood fire. Because hardwood charcoal burns hotter and longer than other fuels, it is excellent for cooking a whole suckling pig or any food that requires more than 45 minutes on the grill. A mesquite charcoal fire can be kept going for hours simply by adding a few live coals to the fire periodically.

Mesquite charcoal is also an imaginative chef's delight, since wonderful fragrances can be created by combining the charcoal with oak, hickory, apple, or other woods. Or you can toss lemon and orange peels, garlic cloves, dried fennel, and fresh herbs such as rosemary or thyme on the coals to produce other pleasing aromas. To intensify the mesquite flavor, simply add wet chips or dry chunks to the fire.

A word of warning: Mesquite charcoal fires tend to give off showers of powerful sparks that sometimes resemble miniature Roman candles. Although these sparks look beautiful

■ *EUREKA!*
"Once fire was recognized, man's instinct for self-improvement led him to subject meat to it, at first to dry out the flesh and finally to place it upon the embers to cook. . . .

"However, it soon became obvious that meat cooked upon live coals is not free from dirt. This inconvenience was remedied by impaling morsels of flesh on sticks which were then placed above the glowing fire.

"It is thus that men hit upon the various methods of grilling, which is a process as simple as it is delicious."
—Jean Anthelme Brillat-Savarin, The Physiology of Taste.

against an evening sky, they can be dangerous. A few years ago Chez Panisse suffered serious damage when mesquite sparks landed in a tinder box next to the grill and set the kitchen afire in the early hours of the morning. When using mesquite charcoal—or the wood, for that matter—move the grill away from dry grass, low-hanging eaves, or any flammable material, including the sack of fuel itself. Keep a pail of water or a spray bottle handy to douse any unexpected flare-ups.

The following chart is a guide that will help you decide whether to use mesquite wood chunks, chips, or pure charcoal with whatever is on the menu. The recommendations are based on flavor and cooking time. Flavor is, of course, a very subjective matter, and you may decide that you like your steak best cooked over mesquite charcoal, or your shrimp strongly flavored with the aroma of smoky wood chips. As the Chinese philosopher Lu Yu wrote, "Taste is for the mouth to decide."

■ EXCELLENT   ◨ GOOD   □ NOT RECOMMENDED

FOOD	CHUNKS	CHARCOAL	CHARCOAL WITH CHUNKS	CHARCOAL WITH WET CHIPS
Steak	■	◨	■	◨
Hamburgers	■	◨	■	◨
Brisket	□	◨	◨	■
Veal	■	◨	■	□
Liver	■	◨	■	◨
Chicken	■	◨	■	◨
Poussin	■	◨	■	◨
Squab	■	◨	■	◨
Duck	■	◨	■	◨

How to Cook with Mesquite Wood and Charcoal

■ EXCELLENT   ◧ GOOD   □ NOT RECOMMENDED

FOOD	CHUNKS	CHARCOAL	CHARCOAL WITH CHUNKS	CHARCOAL WITH WET CHIPS
Pork Ribs	■	◧	■	■
Pork Loin/Butt	◧	◧	■	■
Pork Chops	■	◧	■	■
Lamb	□	■	◧	◧
Kid	◧	■	■	□
Oysters	◧	■	■	□
Lobster	◧	■	■	□
Shrimp	■	◧	■	◧
Swordfish	◧	◧	■	◧
Red Snapper	◧	■	■	□
Tuna	◧	◧	■	◧
Salmon	■	◧	■	◧
Turkey	□	◧	■	■
Pheasant	■	◧	■	■
Quail	■	◧	■	■
Venison	■	◧	■	■
Wild Duck	◧	◧	■	■
Potatoes	■	◧	■	◧
Corn	■	■	■	□
Eggplant	■	◧	■	◧
Squash	■	◧	■	◧
Mushrooms	■	◧	■	□
Red Pepper	■	◧	■	□
Beans	◧	◧	■	■

THE FARMER'S FRIEND
Farmers once considered mesquite a harbinger of spring. So rarely did the tree put out new leaves until the danger of frost was past that a saying arose, "The mesquite knows" (when the winter is done).

This is in direct contrast to the redbud, whose leaves were so often nipped by the frost that the Cherokee word for the tree was "liar."

A sturdy *covered grill* is one of the few essentials for successful mesquite cookery. If you do your cooking over an open fire, the fragrance of the burning wood will simply float off into the air. A covered grill, on the other hand, will hold the aroma under the hood, so that the smoke created when fat and juices drop onto the hot coals can penetrate the food as it cooks.

Covered grills have other distinct advantages. They tend to circulate hot air under the hood much like a convection oven, so that food cooks more evenly and often more quickly. Many grills have adjustable vents that permit you to control the amount of oxygen that reaches the coals—and, consequently, the heat of the fire. This can be a lifesaver if, for example, a grilled chicken begins to scorch on the outside before it is done on the inside. Finally, you can extinguish live coals and save them for another day simply by covering the grill and closing the vents.

Crestline, Meco, W. C. Bradley, and Weber-Stephen manufacture durable covered grills that can stand up to the heat of a mesquite fire. Grills produced by Crestline, Meco, and Bradley feature adjustable fireboxes that let the cook move the heat source closer to or farther away from the food. In the Weber Kettle, food is placed on a grill 4 to 5 inches above the coals, which, in turn, rest on a stationary grate. With practice, you can cook food beautifully on either type of grill, so the choice is really up to you.

If you're a city dweller and your outdoor cooking is limited to a rooftop hibachi, or if you've built an uncovered drop-in grill on your patio, don't despair. You can create a makeshift cover out of several layers of heavy-duty aluminum foil. Be sure to leave enough room under the foil for the air to circulate and a small vent so that the coals can get enough oxygen. With this method, you can experiment with grilling steaks, chicken parts, fish fillets, and vegetables over a mesquite fire. It is not recommended, however, for cooking whole turkeys or any other food that must be cooked covered for more than an hour. Eventually, if you become addicted to mesquite cookery, you will probably want to invest in the convenience of a real covered grill.

Although no other special equipment is necessary, here are a few gadgets that will simplify your life as a mesquite grill chef:

Firestarters. If you're going to the effort of using wood or pure charcoal, don't spoil the fire's wonderful aroma with the chemical odor of lighter fluid. Most mesquite chunks and charcoal can easily be lit using tightly twisted or crumpled newspaper and a few sticks of kindling.

However, there are other options. An electric firestarter, the choice of many professional grill chefs, is a clean, efficient, and relatively quick way of getting a fire lit. You simply plug in the starter, pile mesquite chunks or charcoal on top of the heating element, and wait for the flames to appear. The only real drawback is that the grill must be located near an electrical outlet.

Mesquite charcoal can be started in a metal chimney, or flue. Since most chimneys are designed for uniformly sized briquets, you must be sure to put only larger chunks of charcoal in the chimney. Smaller pieces will slip through the grate and smother the flames. This type of lighting device is also handy for heating up extra coals when grilling foods that require an hour or more cooking time.

You might also consider starting your fire with fatwood kindling, which is now sold through many catalogs and in some gourmet food stores. A few sticks of this resin-impregnated wood will get a merrily blazing fire going within 3 or 4 minutes. Although fatwood has a strong, pitch-scented odor when it burns, the sticks are consumed so quickly by a mesquite fire that the smell dissipates long before you're ready to cook.

Long-handled tongs are useful for turning steaks, chicken parts, whole quail, or small whole fish on the grill. Unlike a fork, they don't pierce the meat and let juices run out. Tongs are also handy for moving hot coals around the grill.

A *long-handled fork* is an aid to roasting sweet peppers over

■ *MUTT AND JEFF*
Mesquite comes two ways. One is "switch" mesquite, which looks more like a bush than a tree— the kind that mostly grows underground, giving the West the reputation of being "a hell of a place where you have to dig for wood and climb for water."

But other mesquite trees have a regal bearing. In northern Mexico, 20-feet trees with trunks a yard in diameter are not uncommon. But the world's record may be held by "Old Geronimo," an Arizona mesquite whose trunk was nearly 15 feet around.

an open flame. Simply impale the pepper on the fork and hold it in the fire until the skin is blackened and blistered all over.

Heatproof barbecue mitts keep fingers from getting scorched when turning metal skewers or when lifting a hot grill to replenish the coals underneath.

A *flat metal spatula* is useful for turning delicate fish steaks and fillets without causing them to fall apart on the grill.

Metal or aluminum foil drip pans are handy for catching juices and fat when grilling chicken, pork spareribs, and other fatty foods by the indirect method.

A *natural bristle basting brush* makes basting with oil or leftover marinade easy. It's also a simple way to oil the grill before cooking.

Metal skewers are safer and sturdier than the thin bamboo variety, which may catch fire when exposed to mesquite's fiery coals. If you do use wooden skewers, be sure to soak them in water before putting them on the grill.

A *wire brush* helps to remove grease and encrusted food from the grill. Make it easy on yourself and clean the grill when it's still warm instead of waiting until the next time you want to use it.

So here you are on a balmy summer evening. Your grill is clean and well oiled. A sack of mesquite wood or perhaps charcoal stands at the ready. A dozen magnificent Hawaiian prawns are soaking up a flavorful marinade of olive oil, lime juice, and cilantro in the kitchen. Your guests have arrived, and the tinkle of ice cubes and light conversation have created an easy, relaxed mood. Everyone is anticipating a wonderful outdoor supper, as you move to light the fire—

It is at this moment that the novice mesquite chef panics. Up till now you've been using easy-to-light charcoal briquets liberally doused with lighter fluid. How on earth will you get these oddly shaped pieces of wood or lumps of charcoal to catch fire?

In fact, starting a mesquite fire is very easy if you have a little patience and follow a few simple tips.

To light a mesquite fire, you can use:

1 An electric starter. Put the starter in the bottom of the grill. Build a small pyramid of 8 to 10 wood chunks and a few smaller pieces of kindling on top of the heating element. Plug in the starter. In 4 or 5 minutes, the chunks will catch fire. Let them burn a few minutes longer or until the wood begins to crackle and pop before removing the element.

2 Newspaper. Tear 4 or 5 sheets of newspaper in half. Twist or crumple them tightly and put the paper in the bottom of the grill. Place 8 to 10 chunks of wood on top with a few smaller pieces of kindling underneath and light the paper with a match. The wood will begin to flame within 7 or 8 minutes. (Hint: If your grill has vents in the bottom, open them. The rush of air will fan the burning newspaper and help the wood to catch fire.)

3 Fatwood kindling. Place 2 sticks of fatwood crisscross in the bottom of the grill. Build a pyramid of 8 to 10 chunks of mesquite wood on top and add a few smaller pieces for kindling. Ignite the ends of the fatwood sticks with a match. The mesquite wood will begin to blaze within 4 or 5 minutes.

A SURVIVOR
Mesquite's deep-diving taproot can find water that lies 50 or 60 feet underground. This lets the tree thrive in places like California's Death Valley, where temperatures of 134° F vaporize everyday plants.

Once a mesquite wood fire is lit, let it burn for a few minutes before adding enough chunks to build up a strong bed of coals. The number of chunks will vary depending on the size of your grill and the amount of food you intend to cook. Until you become adept in mesquite wood cookery, it's better to build too hot a fire and let it burn down than to try to grill over a small fire that is cooling too rapidly.

When can you start cooking over a wood fire? When the flames are low and the coals are red-hot, usually 25 to 30 minutes after the wood first begins to blaze. Spread the coals into a single layer—closely packed together for intense heat or spread apart for a more moderate temperature. Then put the grill in place and start cooking. Because smaller pieces of wood tend to burn up fairly quickly, you may not have enough heat to finish if you wait until the flames have completely died out. The exception, of course, would be if you're grilling shrimp, thin chicken cutlets, or any other food that requires only a short cooking time.

To light a mesquite charcoal fire, you can use:

1 An electric starter. Place the heating element in the bottom of the grill and pile as much mesquite charcoal as you intend to use on top. Plug in the starter. The charcoal will begin to flame within 6 or 7 minutes. Let it burn for a few more minutes and then remove the starter.

2 Newspaper. Tear 4 or 5 sheets of newspaper in half. Twist or crumple them tightly and put them in the bottom of the grill. Pile all the charcoal you think you'll need on top of the paper. (Hint: Don't dump charcoal out of the sack onto the paper. The coal dust seems to keep it from burning well.) Ignite the paper with a match. Within 7 or 8 minutes, the charcoal will catch fire.

3 A metal chimney, or flue. Place an 8-inch square of aluminum foil or a metal drip pan in the bottom of the grill. Crumple 2 or 3 sheets of newspaper and place them on the foil. Put the chimney on top of the newspaper. Fill the top of

the chimney with fairly large pieces of mesquite charcoal. (Smaller pieces will slip through the grate and keep the newspaper from burning properly.) Ignite the newspaper with a match. Within 2 to 3 minutes, the charcoal will begin to glow. Let it burn 5 or 6 minutes longer, or until the bottom of the top layer of charcoal is glowing red. Carefully remove the foil or drip pan and empty the coals into the center of the grill. Add as much charcoal as necessary for the amount of food you intend to cook. Depending on the quantity of charcoal, the coals should be ready within 15 to 20 minutes.

When can you start cooking over a mesquite charcoal fire? When the coals are red-hot and covered with a thin coating of white ash, usually 25 minutes after the charcoal first catches fire. If you're cooking delicate foods such as oysters or lobster, it is advisable to wait until the coals are a little cooler and covered with a layer of gray ash.

If you plan to combine mesquite charcoal with dry wood chunks, mix them when you build the fire and ignite them at the same time. If you intend to add wet mesquite chips to the fire, be sure to put them in water to soak before you start the fire. If they don't absorb enough moisture, they'll burn up instead of smoking. Place them on hot coals just before you're ready to cook.

COOKING TIMES

There are a host of factors that can drastically affect the time it takes to cook food over mesquite wood or charcoal—among them the size of your grill, the size of the fire, and the quantity of food that is being cooked at any one moment. A single skewer of shrimp, for example, may be done to perfection in 4 to 5 minutes, whereas 6 skewers may well need double that time.

Temperature, humidity, and wind can have an equally profound effect upon your fire. A wood fire may burn very hot and fast on a dry autumn day with a brisk wind blowing. But on a muggy summer afternoon, a similar fire might hiss and sputter for 10 to 15 minutes before reluctantly bursting into flame. Add to that the variable quality of mesquite wood and charcoal sold by dozens of small suppliers scattered across the country, and you have a real quandary.

Because there are so many variables, it is a good idea to use the specified cooking time in each recipe as an approximate guide rather than canon law. Over time, you'll become familiar with mesquite wood and charcoal and the peculiarities of your own grill, and if necessary, learn to adjust the indicated times to fit the circumstances.

Each of the following chapters includes specific cooking techniques for different kinds of food. But if you don't want to wade through those instructions, here's a short list of pointers that will make grilling over mesquite wood and charcoal easier.

1 Use a covered grill so that the mesquite aroma can penetrate the food as it cooks.

2 An electric firestarter is the simplest and surest way to ignite the fire.

3 Always start the fire at least 40 minutes before you plan to begin cooking.

4 Be sure that your grill is scrupulously clean and well oiled.

5 Always let food come to room temperature before putting it on the grill. A very light coating of oil helps to keep meat and fish juicy and tender.

6 Let the grill heat up before you put the food on it.

7 Use a hotter fire to grill steaks, pork and veal chops, hamburgers, liver, boneless chicken breasts, shrimp, fish steaks, and fillets. Raise the heat of the fire by packing the coals closely together and opening the vents in the grill.

8 Use a cooler fire to grill lobsters, oysters, clams, vegetables, and butterflied game birds. Lower the heat of the fire by spreading the coals farther apart and closing the vents in the grill.

9 Cook fatty foods such as pork ribs, chicken, and duck and those that require a lengthy cooking time such as turkey or

Continued on next page

■ *HOMESICKNESS*
"One of the preachers got up and gave a big talk on why the mesquites and the prickly pears have thorns on them and why the river comes down occasionally and tears up trees. Sin in this sin-cursed world, he said, is responsible for these things. He did not stop to explain why thorns are sinful, but in heaven, he assured us, there will be no mesquites or prickly pears. 'Man,' I said to myself, 'I sure will get homesick for Texas.'"
—J. Frank Dobie, quoting a letter from "a very intelligent ranch boy," in "Mesquite."

pork loin over a drip pan with coals arranged on either side of the pan.

10 Remember that the quality of the food and ingredients you use will directly affect your results. Whenever possible, try to use only the very best beef, pork, and lamb, the freshest seafood, the tenderest vegetables, and chemical-free chickens and fowl. Fresh herbs are available year-round in many markets. Freshly ground spices, top-quality oils and vinegars, and good wines will also enhance what you cook.

WINES WITH MESQUITE-GRILLED FOODS by Gerald Asher, Wine Editor, *Gourmet*.

Cooking over wood or charcoal in the great outdoors carries such associations of lusty appetites defeating the elements that, for many, the thought of a glass of fine—or any—wine doesn't immediately complete the picture.

Yet at a friend's ranch in Texas recently we drank Château Haut-Brion 1971 with a cauldron of beans and a wild pig that had been spit-turned over mesquite coals since early that morning. Though there was beer for those who preferred it, activity around the ice chest that evening was not particularly brisk.

My 80-year-old Beaujolais godmother, Yvonne Geoffray, has cooked over wood in her kitchen all her life (what would she make of mesquite, I wonder?). She cooks steaks from the Charolais beef raised in the Beaujolais back country right before our eyes in the stone fireplace of the damask-paneled dining room of her snug, ancient house. Bundles of dried vine cuttings burn there as we dip into our soup, and the meat, caught in those French wire contraptions, goes straight onto, indeed into, the embers. We wash it down with the beaming and fragrant Côte de Brouilly from her vineyard outside.

Inside or outside, at a bench or at a table, wine adds immeasurably to the satisfaction of all grilled food, and there are combinations and variations to please everyone.

Flavor expands the "feel" of food and wine, whether red, white, or rosé. (Colette's wine of "pomegranate color" on page 26 was probably a rosé of Tavel.) Regardless of subtleties, and no matter whether they were plainly and naturally sealed in, enhanced with a marinade, or imbued with the smoke of wet chips, the flavors of mesquite-grilled food are bold and need equally direct and robust qualities in the wines that accompany them. As our successful combination of grilled pork and Haut-Brion shows, neither direct nor robust need be taken as a euphemism for something coarse and chewy; the piquancy of marinades and of the peppers, onions, and cilantro so liberally used needs to be accommodated rather than challenged. The intense green-leaf flavor of many Sauvignon

Blancs, for example, or the assertive grapiness of some young California reds will not be at peace with even the simplest grilled fish or meat, while the breadth of a moderately oak-aged Chardonnay, or the discreet strength of a Zinfandel aged a year or two in bottle will work wonders with it.

Courtenay Beinhorn has been careful to recommend a cooking technique appropriate to each type of food, and in the end it is the technique used as much as the actual fish, meat, or fowl that dictates the kind of wine that will best be enjoyed with it—just as, in cooking generally, it is more often the sauce or garnish than the chicken, say, or the sole that must be appropriately matched. That said, I must also say that there is no absolute standard by which wine and food combinations can be judged; some are more acceptable than others among a particular group, in a particular place, at a particular time. If your choice ever seems bizarre to others, remember that someone has to keep pushing at the boundaries. How can we be sure a match won't work if we never try it?

Red wines, especially those most likely to be appreciated with grills, will be softer and more flavorful if decanted before use (for the purpose, a clean bottle or a jug will do just as well as a fine decanter). White wines with the body and flavor needed for grilled foods should not be overchilled. Cool them to roughly 50°F to 55°F, and then keep them in an insulating holder rather than on ice.

Here are recommendations linked to the recipes in this book.

■ *BEEF.* Nothing can beat the frank taste of a California Zinfandel with a grilled steak or a succulent hamburger. But equally good are the red wines of Rioja, the Gran Coronas wines of the Torres family in the Penedès region of Spain, the reds of the southern Rhône in France (try Gigondas, Lirac, and Côtes du Rhône-Villages—they are less expensive than Châteauneuf-du-Pape), and the new Rosso di Montalcino. The last is really the currently fashionable Brunello di Montalcino that has been aged in barrel for less time than the law requires.

WINES WITH MESQUITE-GRILLED FOODS

If anything, it is often more vigorous and more appealing.

The veal chop with mushroom stuffing would take one of the delicious Pinot Noirs being produced so successfully in Oregon and in cooler sections of California. There are new ones breaking through all the time, but you can rely on Eyrie Vineyards from Oregon, and on Acacia Winery, Chalone Vineyard and the Calera Wine Company, among others, in California.

Barbecue sauce, even when cooked on a beef brisket, can make a stout wine seem wispy. This is definitely a time for accommodation rather than challenge—a wine that will charm rather than oppose. Try Preston Vineyards' Gamay Beaujolais from Dry Creek Valley or a wine from one of the Beaujolais crus (Moulin-à-Vent, Fleurie, Chénas, etc.). What is needed is a simple but intense and lasting flavor without the tannin of heavier red wines.

■ *FOWL.* The chicken dishes need the direct flavor of California Chardonnay, but with the poussins I would try Pinot Gris, now being produced in Oregon, or a New York State Seyval aged in oak (Wagner Vineyards produces one). Whites from Europe are tricky with this kind of dish. Those with the right structure (bigger white Burgundies from Meursault and the Montrachet villages, for example, as opposed to Chablis or Mâcon wines), when mature enough, usually have subtleties that could be lost against the marinades and salsas. Pojer & Sandri, odd-named growers in Italy's Alto Adige near the Austrian border, make a Müller-Thurgau that has such flavor that its delicate structure would not be a problem. With this wine, what is more, you will not have to play "hunt the bouquet" in the open air. It will find you.

Chicken livers, I find, are best matched to a zesty, light red wine. I sometimes serve them as a first course when I want a light red rather than a white wine to prepare the way for a special bottle. As a tribute to the mesquite of Texas, I suggest Fall Creek Vineyards' red Carnelian or a young Chianti with the chicken livers and morels. Rosemary overwhelms most white

wines, so I would suggest a Chianti with the squab and rosemary, too. The wine growers of Chianti, like all Tuscans, are so fond of eating small birds that they even have a special way of cooking veal escallops, rolled on picks, that they call "tordi findi"—false thrushes.

The duck breasts will be subtly aromatic, on the other hand, and a perfect foil for a spicy California Cabernet Sauvignon.

■ *PORK, LAMB, AND KID.* Cabernet Sauvignon, as well as red Bordeaux, will also go well with the lamb dishes. Bordeaux and lamb make a classic combination, of course, and I think most Bordeaux will take even a barbecue sauce glaze in stride. The spicy yoghurt and cucumber lamb, on the other hand, is too exotic for Cabernet Sauvignon or Bordeaux and is a dish for which Colette, I suspect, would have pulled one of her full-bodied, dry rosés on us. Be careful: Most rosés are sweet or excessively fruity, and they won't do. Tavel is always dry and full, and there are also dry, well-flavored rosés from Lirac, in the same southern Rhône region, and from Bandol, closer to the coast.

Pork chops and fennel make a wonderfully subtle combination, and I recommend for it a soft, ripe Burgundy, one of the Pinot Noirs I have already mentioned, or a Merlot from California or from the Friuli in northeast Italy. The other pork dishes could be safely matched to even the most chaste of red Bordeaux if it weren't for the tantalizing jellies and sauces. I would prefer for them one of the dry Chenin Blancs of California—Chappellet Vineyard makes an excellent one, as does Martin Brothers Winery in Paso Robles. Slightly hot, slightly sweet, or sweet-sharp flavors need a wine that hangs together well, saying little. For similar reason, I find that a well made dry Chenin Blanc goes best, overall, with most Chinese food.

■ *SEAFOOD.* Many years ago I found that friends in the south of France regularly served red wine with fish whenever there was rouille or aioli served with it. The garlic, they told me, gave it scale. I find I can do the same thing (though I choose a light red wine for the purpose, usually) when I bake salmon

in foil with a layer of finely minced ginger under the fish. I would almost certainly serve red rather than white wines with Courtenay Beinhorn's tuna, snapper, and swordfish dishes, with a preference for a light Bordeaux, a young Beaujolais, or a red Sancerre. If I wanted a white, it would have to be one that could balance the expanded flavors of ginger and garlic without fighting them. Gavi, a white wine from northern Italy, might do it, or a white Graves from Bordeaux with a year or two of bottle age to acquire depth.

Barrel-aged Sauvignon Blanc (sometimes labelled Fumé Blanc) from California will also work if the varietal flavor is subdued. Simi Winery, St. Clement Vineyards, Silverado Vineyards and Robert Mondavi are among those who make their wine in this style.

The oyster, lobster, and prawn dishes will be best with Chardonnay (remember there are some good wines produced in the Finger Lakes, New York, as well as in California), but they will also be delicious with one of the Johannisberg Rieslings of California or Washington State, or a Kabinett wine from Germany.

■ *WILD GAME.* It is with these dishes that I would serve my most prized California Cabernet Sauvignons, special Zinfandels, fine old Rhône wines, and mature Barolos. I would also try some of the new wines coming from Chianti (they are not called Chianti because they use grape combinations not tolerated in the regulations): Sammarco, a Cabernet-based wine from Castello dei Rampolla, for example; Sassicaia, the first Cabernet Sauvignon-based wine to be commercially offered from Tuscany; and Ghiaie della Furba, a wine much like a red Graves, produced by Contini Bonacossi of the Villa di Capezzana. I would play safe with the honey-glazed quail and use a traditional Chianti or a young Beaujolais, however.

But as for venison chili, we'll have to ask Mr. MacLeod what to drink with it. That might expand boundaries for all of us.

BEEF

1 Pick deep red steaks marbled with creamy white fat. Have them cut thick for grilling, 1½ to 3 inches.

2 Let meat come to room temperature before cooking. Refrigerator-cold beef will char on the outside before it gets warm on the inside.

3 Rub steaks with a few drops of extra-virgin olive oil to seal in the juices.

4 Grill steaks 4 to 5 inches from the coals. Turn only once while cooking.

5 Never salt beef until it's off the grill, or the juices will end up in the coals instead of on your plate.

6 Let beef rest before serving, at least 5 minutes.

STEAK WITH GRILLED RED ONIONS AND POBLANO CHILES

Back in the days when cattle roamed the open range, cowboys were meat eaters. No puny filet mignons for them, but great big 7-steaks, fried in their own fat until well done.

Today, our tastes run more to grilling and steaks cooked rare or medium rare, but there's still nothing like mesquite's distinctive aroma to bring out the flavor of prime beef. Slightly charred on the outside and meltingly tender on the inside, these brush country steaks need no embellishment except a little salt and freshly ground pepper. If you must gild the lily, serve them with grilled red onions and poblano chiles—a delicious takeoff on rajitas, the traditional accompaniment of sautéed onions and peppers.

1 Remove the steaks from the refrigerator an hour before cooking so that they can come to room temperature. Trim excess fat. Rub the meat all over with a few drops of olive oil. Sprinkle with freshly ground pepper and press it firmly into the steaks.

2 Slice the onion into rounds about ½ inch thick. Brush with a little olive oil and set aside.

3 Build a fire of mesquite wood. When the flames are high, impale the poblano chiles on a long-handled metal fork and hold them in the fire until the skin is blackened and blistered. Place the chiles in a plastic sack or paper bag. Close the bag tightly and let the chiles steam for 10 minutes. Peel or rub the skins off with your fingers. Remove the stems and seeds, cut the chiles lengthwise into strips, and set aside.

4 When the flames are barely licking over the red-hot coals, place the steaks on the grill and cover. Cook approximately 5 minutes per side for rare, 8 minutes per side for medium, 11 minutes or longer for well done. Turn the steaks only once while cooking.

5 When the steaks are done to taste, remove them from the grill. Place the onion slices on the grill, cover, and cook for 3 to 4 minutes per side or until slightly charred.

6 Serve the steaks, salted to taste, with the grilled chiles and onions on the side.

To serve 4

4 shell steaks, 1½ inches thick

Extra-virgin olive oil

Freshly ground black pepper

4 fresh poblano chiles

2 large red onions

Salt

■ *Beef is the soul of cooking.*
—Marie Antoine Carême

■ *WHAT'S A POBLANO CHILE?*
Poblanos are the temperamental divas of the chile world—some are rather mild; others are ferociously hot. They can be recognized by their dark green color, triangular shape, and oddly twisted surface. Poblanos are usually roasted and peeled before being eaten—or they can be filled with a savory meat and raisin stuffing.

SAN YSIDRO FAJITAS WITH FRESH TOMATO SALSA

To serve 4 to 6

4 pounds skirt steaks

1 cup lime juice

1 large yellow onion

10 garlic cloves

2 or 3 serrano chiles

1 bunch cilantro

Extra-virgin olive oil

Fresh Tomato Salsa
(see recipe, page 116)

12 flour tortillas

The fajita, which in Spanish means "little sash," is better known on this side of the Rio Grande as a skirt steak. South Texas ranchers once considered these long strips of meat from the cow's midsection too tough and stringy for their own tables, so fajitas became the food of the Mexican vaqueros who worked for them. It was the ranchers' loss, because when these flavorful cuts are tenderized with lime juice and grilled over mesquite, the poor man's "steak" becomes a feast for a king.

1 Trim excess fat from meat and remove muscle fiber. Each fajita should be about ½ to ¾ inch thick in order to cook evenly.

2 To prepare the marinade, thinly slice the onions and mince the garlic and serrano chiles. Remove the stems from the cilantro and chop coarsely. Place 1 layer of fajitas in the bottom of a large glass roasting pan. Pour some of the lime juice over it and add garlic, onion, serrano peppers, and cilantro to taste. Place another layer of meat on top and continue until all the ingredients have been used. Cover and marinate in the refrigerator for 3 to 4 hours.

3 Prepare Fresh Tomato Salsa.

4 Build a fire of mesquite wood in your grill. Remove the fajitas from the marinade, pat dry, and rub with a little olive oil. When the flames are low and the coals are red-hot, place the fajitas on the grill and cover. Cook 3 to 4 minutes per side for rare, or a few minutes longer for medium or well done. Turn the meat only once while cooking.

5 Remove the fajitas from the grill and let them rest on a wooden cutting board for 5 minutes. Sprinkle with salt to taste. Slice on the diagonal and serve on warm flour tortillas with tomato salsa. Be sure to have lots of napkins and plenty of ice-cold beer on hand.

FLANK STEAK IN RED WINE WITH LEEKS AND RED PEPPERS

Here's another version of steak with rajitas. Instead of sautéed onions and chiles, the meat is accompanied by grilled leeks and sweet red peppers. The flank steak itself, first cousin to the skirt steak used in fajitas, is a tasty but often tough cut of beef that yields gracefully to a day-long marinade in red wine and herbs. Consider grilling twice as much as you expect to eat—it's even more delicious for breakfast the next morning.

1 Trim the steak of excess fat and place in it a shallow glass pan. Combine the wine, vinegar, garlic, ¼ cup olive oil, thyme, and pepper and pour the mixture over the meat. Make sure the steak is thoroughly coated on all sides. Marinate in the refrigerator for 6 to 8 hours, turning every hour or so.

2 Combine the crushed garlic clove and 2 tablespoons of olive oil in a small dish and set aside.

3 To prepare the leeks, trim the roots and tops, leaving 3 inches of green above the white bulb. Remove the tough outer leaves. Insert the tip of a sharp paring knife about ½ inch above the bottom of the bulb and slit the leek in half lengthwise. (Do not cut through the bottom of the bulb.) Turn the leek 90 degrees and repeat the process. Hold the leek under running water and rinse the leaves thoroughly to remove grit. Pat dry, brush with olive oil, and set aside.

4 Build a mesquite wood fire in your grill. When the flames are high, impale the red peppers on a long-handled metal fork and hold them in the fire until the skins are blackened and

Continued on next page

To serve 4

2 pounds flank steak

½ cup dry red wine

2 tablespoons balsamic vinegar

1 teaspoon minced garlic

¼ cup extra-virgin olive oil

2 tablespoons fresh thyme, minced

Freshly cracked black pepper

1 clove garlic, crushed

2 tablespoons extra-virgin olive oil

4 small sweet red peppers

8 small leeks

2 tablespoons lemon juice

Salt

■ *WHAT'S A SERRANO CHILE?*
The serrano is a smooth, medium-green chile that is smaller and skinnier than the jalapeño. Used only fresh, it packs a wallop and is used to add fire to fresh salsas and marinades.

■ *"Charbonadoes, or carbonadoes, is meat broyled upon the coals, of divers kinds according to men's pleasures."*
—Gervase Markham, The English Housewife, 1649

FLANK STEAK IN RED WINE
WITH LEEKS AND RED PEPPERS *Continued*

blistered. Put the peppers in a plastic bag or paper sack. Close the sack tightly and let the peppers steam for 10 minutes. Peel or rub the skins off with your fingers. Remove the stems and seeds and cut the peppers into thin strips. Drizzle with the garlic-flavored olive oil, sprinkle with lemon juice, and set aside.

5 When the coals are red-hot and the flames are low, put the steak and the leeks on the grill and cover. Cook the meat 4 to 5 minutes, then turn and cook another 4 minutes for rare. For medium rare, cook 5 to 6 minutes per side. Grill the leeks until they are soft and slightly charred.

6 Remove the steaks and leeks from the grill. Let the steak rest for 10 minutes on a wooden chopping block. To serve, slice very thinly on the diagonal. Sprinkle with salt to taste. Garnish with 2 leeks and a tangle of red peppers.

FILET STUFFED WITH SUN-DRIED TOMATOES, PINE NUTS AND CAPERS

A beef filet grilled over mesquite is an impressive centerpiece for a festive outdoor dinner. In this recipe, piquant sun-dried tomatoes and capers beautifully underscore the slightly smoky flavor of the meat.

1 Sauté the pine nuts in 1 tablespoon olive oil until golden. Set aside.

2 Butterfly the filet by cutting a 2-inch-deep slit the length of the filet. Open it up and place 1 layer of sun-dried tomatoes on the bottom half of the meat, keeping the tomatoes at least ½ inch from the edge. Top with pine nuts and capers and another layer of tomatoes. Stitch the filet closed with a needle and heavy thread and tie it at 1-inch intervals with kitchen string. Rub the filet all over with a little olive oil, sprinkle with pepper to taste, and set aside.

3 Build a fire of ½ mesquite wood and ½ mesquite charcoal. When the coals are red-hot and covered with white ash, place the filet in the center of the grill and cover. Cook for approximately 30 minutes until medium rare, turning every 5 or 6 minutes.

4 When done, remove the filet from the grill and let it rest for 10 minutes. Carve into 1-inch-thick slices and serve.

To serve 4

2 tablespoons pine nuts

1 tablespoon extra-virgin olive oil

2½ pounds filet of beef, in 1 piece

8 to 10 sun-dried tomatoes in olive oil

1 tablespoon capers

Extra-virgin olive oil

Freshly ground black pepper

MORE WAYS TO STUFF A FILET

With sautéed shiitake mushrooms and onions.

With sautéed poblano chiles, onions, garlic, and white cheddar cheese, as they do at Cafe Marimba in New York.

With a few sprigs of fresh herbs, such as marjoram or thyme, and roasted red and yellow peppers.

HAMBURGERS WITH CHUNKY GUACAMOLE

To serve 4

1½ pounds freshly ground sirloin

Salt and freshly ground black pepper

4 soft rolls

2 firm, ripe Haas avocados

1 medium tomato, finely chopped

1 small red onion, finely chopped

1 small bunch cilantro, finely chopped

Juice of 1 lime

Salt

Sweet butter

Hamburgers grilled over a mesquite wood fire make a simple, eminently satisfying outdoor supper. The aroma of the smoldering coals brings out the natural flavor of top-quality ground sirloin so beautifully that you need add only freshly ground black pepper and a little salt to taste.

If possible, have the butcher grind the meat for you—or do it yourself. The difference between freshly ground beef and the packaged variety that has been sitting around in the supermarket for a few days is like the difference between a Mercedes-Benz and a Chevrolet—they'll both get you there, but. . . .

Mesquite-grilled hamburgers are delicious served with a chunky version of the classic Mexican guacamole—chopped-up avocado (preferably the black-skinned, buttery-tasting Haas variety), tomato, and red onion, flavored with lime juice and cilantro. If you can find freshly baked soft rolls, so much the better—they are superior to ordinary hamburger buns and make a perfect topping for this easy supper dish.

1 Mix the ground sirloin with salt and freshly ground black pepper to taste. Shape the meat into patties about ½ inch thick. Split the rolls in half.

2 Build a fire of mesquite wood chunks. While the fire is burning, prepare the guacamole: Peel and seed the avocados and chop them into small cubes. Put the avocado in a bowl and add tomato, onion, cilantro, lime juice, and salt to taste. Stir well, taste, and correct seasonings. Set aside.

3 When the flames are low and the coals are red-hot, put the meat patties on the grill and cover. Cook 4 minutes. Turn the patties and place the rolls at the outer edges of the grill to warm them. Cook the patties for 4 minutes more until medium rare.

4 When the hamburgers are done, remove them from the grill. Spread the rolls with butter, place the patties on top, and serve with a bowl of chunky guacamole on the side.

BARBECUED BEEF BRISKET

Brisket slow-cooked over glowing mesquite coals is a Texas barbecue classic. Although authentic barbecue is cooked in pits for 8 to 10 hours, you can get nearly the same effect by using mesquite charcoal and a covered grill. The secret is to maintain a slow, steady heat by partly closing the vents on the grill and replenishing the fire with live coals every hour or so. Brisket must be cooked for at least 5 hours—even a little longer if you can manage it—so plan to spend the day around the house, working up an appetite by reading a good book like Ramon Adams' *Come an' Get It,* while you tend the grill.

An hour before the brisket is done, add wet mesquite chips to the fire for extra flavor, and brush the meat with Easy Tomato-Jalapeño Barbecue Sauce. Or use your own favorite sauce. Either way, the results can't help but please.

1 Rub the brisket all over with olive oil. Mix the dry spices together and rub them into the meat and fat.

2 Put 4 cups of mesquite wood chips in water to soak. Build a good-sized fire of mesquite charcoal. When the coals are medium-hot and covered with grayish ash, divide them in half and push them to opposite sides of the grill. Put an aluminum foil drip pan in the center. Place the brisket on the grill and cover. Partly close the dampers to control the burning.

Cook the meat for 4 hours. Every 50 to 60 minutes, turn the meat and check the coals. If the fire is too cool, add 3 or 4 live, medium-sized coals to each side of the drip pan and

Continued on next page

To serve 6

4 pounds beef brisket, in 1 piece

1 tablespoon extra-virgin olive oil

¾ teaspoon freshly ground black pepper

¾ teaspoon freshly ground white pepper

½ teaspoon paprika

½ teaspoon ground cumin

½ teaspoon salt

Easy Tomato-Jalapeño Barbecue Sauce (see recipe, page 39)

■ *HOW TO DRESS UP A MESQUITE-GRILLED HAMBURGER*

1. Brush the hamburger patties with Easy Tomato-Jalapeño Barbecue Sauce (see recipe, page 39) just before the meat is done. Sprinkle with chopped onion.

2. Top with a red wine-herb butter. Over high heat, reduce ½ cup dry red wine, 1 tablespoon minced shallots, and ½ teaspoon black pepper to 2 tablespoons. Beat the mixture into ½ cup sweet butter until fluffy. Stir in 1 tablespoon mixed herbs such as marjoram, thyme, and parsley. Set aside for 1 hour to let the flavors mingle.

3. Top with a generous spoonful of Quick Four-Pepper Relish (see recipe, page 122).

open the dampers slightly. (Start extra coals in a small brazier, charcoal chimney lighter, or flowerpot.) If the fat in the drip pan is sizzling, the fire may be too hot—close the dampers slightly to control the heat. Your objective is to achieve a slow, steady heat.

3 While the brisket is cooking, prepare Easy Tomato-Jalapeño Barbecue Sauce.

4 After 4 hours, open the dampers and replenish the coals. Place 2 cups of wet mesquite chips over the coals. Brush the brisket all over with barbecue sauce and cover. Cook for 30 minutes. If necessary, add more wet mesquite chips to the fire, but not so many that they extinguish the coals. Turn the brisket and brush again with barbecue sauce. Cover and cook for a final 30 minutes.

5 Remove the brisket from the grill and let it rest for 10 minutes. Carve it against the grain in thin slices and serve with a big pot of beans, your favorite coleslaw, and a bowl of warm barbecue sauce on the side.

Easy Tomato-Jalapeño Barbecue Sauce

This is a simple barbecue sauce that can be assembled in a few minutes and then left to simmer on the back burner while you go about tending the fire. Since tomato-based sauces tend to burn, wait until you've almost finished cooking before brushing it on the meat. It's good with hamburgers, chicken, brisket, and pork.

1 Combine all the ingredients in a nonaluminum saucepan. Simmer over low heat for 50 minutes. If the mixture begins to get too thick, add a little more water.

2 Remove the sauce from the heat and let it cool slightly. If you prefer a smooth sauce, pour it through a strainer and press on the solids with the back of a wooden spoon. Otherwise, it's ready to use. The sauce will keep for at least a week in the refrigerator.

Makes about 2 cups

3 cups ketchup

2 cups water

1 cup finely chopped onion

3 tablespoons Worcestershire sauce

2 tablespoons soy sauce

1 tablespoon cider vinegar

1 tablespoon brown sugar

2 teaspoons ground ginger

1½ teaspoons ground cumin

2 teaspoons dry mustard

2 tablespoons finely chopped garlic

2 or more canned jalapeños, seeded and finely chopped

1 tablespoon extra-virgin olive oil

FOURTH OF JULY BARBECUE
Cabrito with Cumin and Pequín Chiles (page 58).
Tart Tomatillo Sauce (page 118).
Warm Corn Tortillas.
Tossed Green Salad.
Peach Cobbler.

WHAT'S A JALAPEÑO?
Jalapeño peppers are medium-green, smooth-skinned chiles, usually 1½ inches long and ½ inch wide. Fresh, their flavor varies from hot to very hot. Pickled in escabeche, they are hotter still. Jalapeños are used to perk up marinades or to add sting to a sauce.

VEAL CHOPS WITH JALAPEÑO-MUSTARD BUTTER

To serve 4

Jalapeño-mustard butter:

   2 large canned jalapeño peppers

   4 ounces sweet butter, softened

   2 tablespoons Dijon mustard

   1 large clove garlic, minced

4 veal chops, 1¼-inch-thick

2 tablespoons extra-virgin olive oil

2 tablespoons lemon juice

1 teaspoon fresh chopped sage

Salt and freshly ground pepper

Tender, milk-fed veal is delicious when cooked over a mellow mesquite wood and charcoal fire. The spicy jalapeño butter adds a lively, contrasting note.

1 Remove the stems and seeds of the jalapeño peppers and chop very finely. Cream the butter until it is very smooth and beat in the mustard. Add the jalapeño peppers and garlic and blend well. Let the butter stand in a cool spot for at least an hour so that the flavors can mingle.

2 Build a fire of ½ mesquite wood and ½ mesquite charcoal. While the fire is burning, trim the veal chops of any excess fat. Roll the tails in and tie with a piece of string. Rub the veal all over with the olive oil. Sprinkle with lemon juice and chopped sage.

3 When the coals are red-hot and covered with white ash, place the chops on the grill. Cover and cook for 4 to 5 minutes per side, or until they are barely pink in the center.

4 Sprinkle the veal chops with salt and pepper to taste, and serve with a generous dollop of jalapeño-mustard butter on top.

VEAL CHOPS STUFFED WITH SHIITAKE MUSHROOMS

In spring and fall, veal is often served with wild mushrooms. In this recipe, the chops are stuffed with a rich mixture of fresh shiitake and ordinary mushrooms, but fresh morels or chanterelles would be equally delicious. You can also use dried wild mushrooms that have been plumped in warm water.

1 Remove the stems from the mushrooms and reserve for another use. Wipe the caps with a damp cloth. Slice thinly and set aside. (If using dried mushrooms, soak them in hot water for 20 minutes or until soft. Squeeze gently to remove excess water. Remove the stems and slice the caps thinly.)

2 In a large skillet, sauté the shallots in 3 tablespoons of butter over medium-high heat until they turn golden. Add the mushrooms and the rest of the butter and cook over medium heat for another 5 to 6 minutes, or until the mushrooms are very soft. Stir in the parsley. Remove from heat and let cool to room temperature.

3 Using a sharp knife, make a deep horizontal slit in the side of each veal chop. Stuff the pocket with the mushroom mixture. Stitch the slit closed with needle and thread, or secure it with poultry lacing pins. Wrap the tail around the chop and secure with a skewer or lacing pin. Rub the chops all over with olive oil and the cut side of the garlic clove. Sprinkle with salt and pepper to taste.

4 Build a fire of ½ mesquite wood mixed with ½ mesquite charcoal. When the coals are red-hot and the flames are low, put the chops on the grill and cover. Cook for 5 minutes per side for medium rare, or 2 to 3 minutes longer for well done.

5 Remove the chops from the grill and let them rest for 5 minutes. Remove the lacing pins or the thread and serve, garnished with lemon wedges.

To serve 6

¼ pound fresh shiitake mushrooms (or 1 ounce dried)

¼ pound cultivated mushrooms

1½ cups thinly sliced shallots

6 tablespoons sweet butter

2 tablespoons minced parsley

6 veal chops, 1½ inches thick

3 tablespoons extra-virgin olive oil

1 garlic clove, cut in half

6 lemon wedges

■ *WHAT'S A SHIITAKE?*
Shiitake mushrooms, so called because they grow on logs of the shii tree, are widely used in Chinese and Japanese cooking. Once found only in the wild, they are now being cultivated on the West Coast and can be had fresh, for a price, all year-round. Shiitakes make a superb grilling mushroom: Their thick, meaty caps taste a little like beef, and after a few minutes over hot coals, they acquire a delectably smoky flavor.

LIVER WITH SAGE BUTTER AND ROASTED SHALLOTS

To serve 4

Sage butter:

  4 ounces sweet butter, softened

  2 teaspoons lemon juice

  1 tablespoon minced sage

  ¾ teaspoon coarsely ground black pepper

4 slices calf's liver, ½-inch-thick

Extra-virgin olive oil

12 large shallots, unpeeled

Fresh calf's liver grilled over mesquite wood will please even the most ardent liver haters, especially when served with tangy sage butter. Shallots, grilled alongside the liver in their papery skins, become sweet and buttery soft.

1 Cream the butter with a fork until it is very soft and smooth. Beat in the lemon juice until it is absorbed and the butter is fluffy. Add the sage and black pepper and blend well. Let the butter stand in a cool spot for at least an hour so that the flavors can mingle.

2 Brush the calf's liver and unpeeled shallots generously with olive oil and set aside.

3 Build a mesquite wood fire. When the coals are red-hot and the flames are very low, place the shallots on the grill around the edges of the coals. Cover, cook for 4 minutes, and turn. Add the liver to the grill, cover, and cook for 2 minutes. Turn the liver and cook for 2 minutes more. Remove the liver and shallots from the grill.

4 Serve the liver immediately, topped with a generous spoonful of sage butter and the shallots on the side.

PORK

In "A Dissertation Upon Roast Pig," Charles Lamb recounts the surely apocryphal tale of Bo-Bo, the swineherd's idiot son who accidentally burned down the family hut—and in so doing, discovered roast pork. Thereafter, whenever they wanted to feast upon this new taste sensation, the swineherd and his family set fire to their humble abode.

Bo-Bo notwithstanding, there are better ways of grilling pork than burning the house down. Here are a few tips:

1 Pork chops are juiciest when cut 1-inch thick and grilled directly over the coals just until they are no longer pink in the center.

2 Spareribs, whole pork loins, or pork butts—all fattier cuts of meat that require a longer cooking time—should be grilled over a drip pan with hot coals on either side. For the most flavorful results, mix long-lasting mesquite charcoal with aromatic mesquite, hickory, or oak chunks.

3 A whole suckling pig is delectable when spit-roasted outdoors over mesquite logs. Small pigs, no more than 10 to 12 pounds, can be cooked on a covered grill. Slowly cook the pig over medium-hot mesquite charcoal, and turn only once!

4 Let pork come to room temperature before grilling. Rub with extra-virgin olive oil to seal in the juices.

BARBECUED PORK TACOS WITH TWO LIVELY SAUCES

Pork is one of the finest barbecue meats, especially when it is cooked over a mixture of mesquite wood and charcoal. Here, its rich, smoky flavor is set off to perfection by 2 very different sauces: one a sweetly piquant tomato sauce flavored with oranges, the other a fiery vinegar sauce laced with red and black pepper. Served in crispy taco shells topped with one or both sauces, it's a treat for a Saturday night supper with good friends.

1 Prepare Mesquite Barbecue Sauce, Smoky No. 1 and Down East Moppin' and Soppin' Sauce. (This can be done several days in advance.)

2 Butterfly the pork butt by slicing horizontally about ⅔ of the way through the meat as it rests on a wooden cutting board. Open it up so that it lies flat on the surface. Pierce the meat with the tip of a small, sharp knife in a dozen places and insert slivers of garlic. Rub the pork all over with olive oil and sprinkle with salt and pepper to taste.

3 Put 2 cups of mesquite wood chips in water to soak. Build a fire of ⅔ mesquite charcoal and ⅓ mesquite wood. When the flames are low and the coals are red-hot, divide the coals in half and move them to either side of the grill. Place an aluminum drip pan in the center. Scatter a handful of wet mesquite chips on top of the coals. Place the pork on the grill above the drip pan and cover. Cook for 1 hour and 15 minutes, turning

Continued on next page

To serve 6

1½ cups Mesquite Barbecue Sauce, Smoky No. 1 (see recipe, page 119)

1 cup Down-East Moppin' and Soppin' Sauce (see recipe, page 121)

3 pounds fresh pork butt, in 1 piece

1 large clove garlic, slivered

Extra-virgin olive oil

Salt and coarsely ground pepper

3 to 4 cups safflower oil

18 fresh corn tortillas

■ *WHY I LIKE MESQUITE*
"Originally, I was looking for a natural alternative to petroleum by-products. I discovered that mesquite charcoal burns hotter and longer than other woods. It gives a delicious flavor to strong-tasting foods—like rockfish and marinated pork loin or vegetables like eggplant, onions, and leeks."
—Alice Waters, chef and co-owner, Chez Panisse

every 10 to 15 minutes, or until the juices run yellow when the thickest part of the butt is pricked with the tines of a fork.

4 While the pork is cooking, pour ½ inch of safflower oil into a small, cast-iron skillet and heat until it is smoking. Using tongs, drop a tortilla into the oil and quickly fold it in half. Fry the tortilla for 1 to 2 minutes, until it is crisp but not brown. Remove and drain the taco shell on several thick paper towels. Repeat with the rest of the tortillas.

5 When the pork is done, remove it from the grill and let it rest for 10 minutes before carving it into very thin slices. To serve, stuff each taco with 2 or 3 pieces of meat and serve with warm bowls of the 2 barbecue sauces. Delicious with a simple green salad.

BABY BACK RIBS WITH BOURBON-HONEY GLAZE

Baby back ribs are the tenderest, most succulent ribs—and they are the very best for grilling. Here they are brushed with a mellow bourbon and honey glaze and then grilled over mesquite charcoal mixed with hickory wood. The results are superlative.

1 Place the ribs in a shallow glass pan. Combine the rest of the ingredients in a bowl and mix well. Brush the ribs with the bourbon and honey mixture, making sure that all sides are well coated. Let them stand at cool room temperature for 1 to 2 hours.

2 Build a fire of ⅔ mesquite charcoal mixed with ⅓ hickory chunks. When the flames are low and the coals are red-hot, divide them in half and push them to opposite sides of the grill. Place an aluminum drip pan in the center. Sprinkle the ribs with salt and pepper to taste, and place them on the grill directly over the drip pan. Cover and cook for 15 minutes. Turn, baste with the bourbon mixture, and cook another 15 minutes. Turn, baste again, and cook for 5 to 10 minutes longer, or until the ribs are crispy on the outside and the juices run yellow when the thickest part of the meat is pricked with a fork.

3 Remove the ribs from the grill and let them rest for 10 minutes before carving into individual servings. Delicious as is or sprinkled with a few drops of Down East Moppin' and Soppin' Sauce (see recipe, page 121).

To serve 4

3½ pounds baby back ribs

¼ cup bourbon

3 tablespoons honey

1 tablespoon peanut oil

1 tablespoon soy sauce

1 small clove garlic, minced

Salt and freshly ground pepper

MORE RAVE REVIEWS FOR RIBS Grilled ribs are always a crowd-pleaser. Here are 2 more good ways to fix them.

1. Tangy Texas Ribs: Marinate beef ribs in Easy Tomato-Jalapeño Barbecue Sauce (see recipe, page 39) or Mesquite Barbecue Sauce, Smoky No. 1 (see recipe, page 119) for 2 hours. Pat dry, rub with oil, and grill over mesquite. Serve with warm sauce on the side.

2. Oriental Ribs: Marinate pork spareribs in soy sauce, honey, red wine vinegar, ginger, garlic, and scallions for 3 hours. Baste with sauce while grilling over mesquite charcoal.

PORK LOIN WITH PEANUT AND ANCHO CHILE SAUCE

To serve 6

Peanut-Chile Sauce:

8 large dried ancho chiles

¾ cup freshly roasted, unsalted peanuts

2 large cloves garlic

½ teaspoon ground cumin

¾ cup fresh tomato puree

1 cup chopped onion

2 tablespoons extra-virgin olive oil

Salt to taste

3 pounds pork loin, in 1 piece

Extra-virgin olive oil

Salt and freshly ground pepper

The secret of this delicious sauce is to use very freshly roasted peanuts. Coarsely ground and mixed with a puree of mellow ancho chiles, they make a beautiful accompaniment for very simply grilled pork loin. The sauce is also excellent with lamb, kid, and poussin, or baby chicken.

■ Remove the stems and seeds from the ancho chiles and tear them into pieces. Cover with 4 cups boiling water and let them stand for 15 to 20 minutes, or until very soft. Drain, but reserve 3 cups of the soaking liquid.

■ In a blender or food processor, coarsely grind the peanuts and set aside. Place the ancho chiles, garlic, cumin, and 1 cup of the soaking liquid in the blender or food processor and liquefy. Stir in the fresh tomato pureé and set aside.

■ In a saucepan, sauté the onion in olive oil until very brown. Add the chiles and mix well. Heat gently for 10 minutes, adding 1 or more cups soaking liquid if the mixture becomes too thick or begins to stick. Stir in the ground peanuts and heat for 3 minutes longer. Add salt to taste. Remove from heat, but keep warm.

■ Cut the pork loin into slices ¾ inch thick. Rub with olive oil and sprinkle with salt and pepper to taste.

Continued on next page

PORK LOIN WITH PEANUT AND ANCHO CHILE SAUCE

5 Put 2 cups of mesquite wood chips in water to soak. Build a fire of ⅓ mesquite wood and ⅔ mesquite charcoal. When the coals are red-hot and flames are low, scatter a handful of wet mesquite chips on the coals. As soon as the chips begin to smoke, place the pork slices on the grill and cover. Cook for 7 to 8 minutes per side or until no longer pink in the center.

6 When the pork is done, remove it from the grill and let it rest for 2 to 3 minutes. Serve with a bowl of the ancho chile peanut sauce and Roasted Corn with Lime and Pequín Chiles (see recipe, page 102).

WHAT'S AN ANCHO CHILE? The ancho chile is a dried poblano. Very dark, almost ma-hogany colored, the ancho is triangular in shape and quite wrinkled. Its flavor varies from mellow to very hot. Soaked in warm water and puréed, ancho paste forms the base for many delicious sauces and can also be added to chili.

WINTER PORK CHOPS WITH FENNEL

To serve 4

4 center-cut pork chops, 1 inch thick

2 tablespoons extra-virgin olive oil

2 tablespoons lemon juice

Salt and coarsely ground pepper

1 tablespoon minced garlic

1 cup chopped fennel root

8 slices fennel root, ½ inch thick

Extra-virgin olive oil

Fennel, an aromatic winter vegetable, is delicious grilled out-doors over mesquite coals. In this recipe, which is loosely based on one in Elizabeth David's *A Book of Mediterranean Food,* its anise-like flavor makes pork chops marinated in lemon and olive oil taste surprisingly like bacon.

1 Trim excess fat from the chops. Rub them all over with olive oil. Sprinkle both sides with lemon juice, salt, and pepper. Press the garlic and chopped fennel root firmly into the meat. Let the chops stand at cool room temperature for 3 hours.

2 Brush the sliced fennel root with olive oil and set aside.

3 Build a mesquite wood fire. When the flames are low and the coals are red-hot, place the chops on the grill and cover. Cook for 5 minutes. Turn the chops, add the fennel to the grill, and cook for another 5 minutes. Turn the chops and the fennel and cook for a final 5 to 10 minutes, or until the chops are no longer pink in the center. The fennel should be soft and slightly charred.

4 Remove the chops and the fennel from the grill. Let the chops rest for 5 or 6 minutes before serving. Excellent with a salad of bitter greens, such as chicory, arugula, and endive, dressed with a mustard vinaigrette.

WILD SOUTH TEXAS HOG IN ORANGE JUICE AND CHAMPAGNE

Among the curious denizens of the brush country are feral hogs, descendants of domestic pigs who escaped generations back and now run wild through the mesquite thickets. From horseback, you may spy them traveling in herds—tusked boars and fat sows in front, plump piglets trailing behind. If they catch your scent, they'll take off in a cloud of dust, snorting and snuffling, their little hooves pounding.

Feral hogs mostly grub for roots, but they also have an uncanny knack for sniffing out other delicacies. Many a rancher's wife has discovered their telltale tracks around her ravaged vegetable garden, and the hunter is likely to find that the corn he laid out for quail and deer in the evening was devoured by the hogs before morning. In times of drought, they have even been known to feast on mesquite beans.

Whatever their diet, young feral hogs make excellent eating. Their lean and tender flesh has just a hint of gamy flavor. This recipe, which was concocted for a summer barbecue, calls for day-long marinating in orange juice and dry champagne.

1 Using a mortar and pestle, bruise the cumin seed slightly. Combine the orange juice, champagne, garlic, cumin, and orange zest and mix well.

2 Place the ribs in a large, shallow glass roasting pan and pour the orange juice mixture over them. Make sure that the ribs are coated on all sides. Let them stand for 6 hours at cool

Continued on next page

To serve 6

1 tablespoon cumin seed

2 cups freshly squeezed orange juice

1½ cups dry champagne

8 large cloves garlic, chopped

1 tablespoon slivered orange zest

5 pounds wild hog ribs (or substitute baby back ribs)

2 tablespoons safflower oil

Salt and freshly ground pepper

"Never eat more than you can lift."
—Miss Piggy

room temperature or 8 to 10 hours in the refrigerator, turning occasionally.

3 Build a fire of ½ mesquite wood and ½ mesquite charcoal. When the coals are red-hot and the flames are low, move the coals to either side of the grill and place an aluminum drip pan in the center. Remove the ribs from the marinade, pat dry, and rub them with safflower oil. Sprinkle with salt and pepper to taste. Place them on the grill over the drip pan, cover, and cook for 15 minutes. Turn, baste with remaining marinade, and cook for another 15 minutes. Turn, baste again, and cook for a final 5 to 10 minutes. The ribs are done when they are crispy on the outside and the juices run clear when the meat is pricked with the tines of a fork.

4 Remove the ribs from the grill and let them rest on a wooden cutting board for 5 minutes. Carve them into individual servings and serve with plenty of jalapeño jelly and Mimi's Buttermilk Cornbread with Green Chiles (see recipe, page 127).

LAMB AND KID

LAMB WITH PAPAYA AND CILANTRO

To serve 6

1 butterflied leg of lamb,
4 to 5 pounds

2 tablespoons extra-virgin olive oil

Salt and coarsely ground pepper

1½ tablespoons grated lemon zest

4 juniper berries, crushed

2 tablespoons fresh thyme,
chopped

2 tablespoons fresh cilantro,
chopped

3 tablespoons minced shallots

1 tablespoon minced garlic

1 firm, ripe papaya

¼ cup melted butter

A butterflied leg of lamb is especially delicious when grilled outdoors. However, unless you are fond of a very pronounced mesquite taste, it's always best to cook lamb over mesquite charcoal, which has a milder aroma. In this recipe, the exotically flavored lamb is nicely set off by warm slices of sweet papaya.

Using a sharp knife, cut away the excess fat and muscle fiber from the butterflied leg of lamb. Rub the meat all over with olive oil and sprinkle with salt and pepper to taste. Mix the lemon zest, juniper, thyme, cilantro, shallots, and garlic together and rub the mixture well into the meat on both sides. Let the lamb stand at cool room temperature for 3 to 4 hours, or 6 hours in the refrigerator.

Build a mesquite charcoal fire. When the coals are red-hot and the flames are low, put the lamb on the grill and cover. Cook for 8 to 10 minutes per side, or until the lamb is just pink in the thickest part. Grill a few minutes longer if you prefer your lamb well done. Remove the meat from the grill and let it rest for 10 minutes.

Cut the papaya into slices ½ inch thick, remove the seeds, and brush with melted butter. Grill for 2 minutes per side, just long enough to warm it through.

To serve, slice the lamb very thin and serve it with the warm papaya on the side, sprinkled with a little chopped cilantro and lime juice, if desired.

YOGHURT-MARINATED LAMB WITH GREEN CHILES

The British brought mesquite to India in the mid-nineteenth century, principally for use as a livestock feed and a cooking fuel. It quickly became so valuable that in Jodhpur, mesquite was declared the "royal plant," since it supplied the people with a good part of the wood they used in their cooking fires.

Whether the maharajah of Jodhpur ever tasted lamb cooked over mesquite is unknown, but it is true that this dish—which combines boneless lamb chunks with yoghurt, Indian spices, and hot green chiles—is fit for royal princes of any blood. Since the lamb is on the spicy side, serve it with cooling bowls of plain yoghurt and simply sliced tomatoes and cucumbers.

Cut the lamb into 1½-inch chunks.

Combine the yoghurt, garlic, and ginger in a large bowl. In a spice mill or with a mortar and pestle, pulverize the coriander, cumin, and cardamon seeds. Add the spices to the yoghurt mixture and blend well. Add the lamb and toss so that the

Continued on next page

To serve 4

2 pounds boneless lamb

¾ cup plain yoghurt

1 tablespoon minced garlic

1 tablespoon chopped fresh ginger

¼ teaspoon coriander seeds

¼ teaspoon cumin seeds

¼ teaspoon shelled cardamon seeds

Salt

2 tablespoons olive oil

8 to 10 long green hot chiles

BENGALI BANQUET

Yoghurt-Marinated Lamb with Green Chiles (page 55).

Pat's Louisiana Peach Chutney (page 124).

Skewered Onions, Eggplant, and Red Pepper (page 100).

Sliced Cucumbers and Tomatoes with Yoghurt.

Mango Ice Cream Garnished with Slices of Fresh Mango.

meat is thoroughly coated with the mixture. Refrigerate for 8 hours or overnight, turning occasionally.

▣ Remove the lamb from the refrigerator about an hour before you want to begin cooking. Scrape off the excess marinade and thread the lamb onto long metal skewers, alternating with 1 or 2 green chiles. Set aside.

▣ Build a fire of mesquite charcoal. When the coals are red-hot, but no longer flaming, place the lamb on the grill. Cover and cook for 4 to 5 minutes per side, or until the lamb reaches medium rare and is still pink inside.

▣ Remove the skewers from the grill and let the meat rest for 5 minutes. Serve with individual bowls of yoghurt and a cucumber and tomato salad on the side.

HONEY-BASTED RACK OF LAMB

A mesquite-grilled rack of lamb is a wonderful centerpiece for a festive holiday dinner. This subtle lemon, olive oil, and honey baste keeps the meat moist while adding just a hint of flavor. The same baste is very good with venison, quail, and dove.

■ Trim the rack until there is only a thin covering of fat about ⅛ inch thick.

■ Combine the remaining ingredients in a bowl and mix well.

■ Build a mesquite charcoal fire. When the coals are red-hot but no longer flaming, place the rack on the grill fat side down and cover. Cook for 5 minutes. Baste with the lemon-honey mixture, turn, and cook for 10 minutes. Baste again, turn, and cook for a final 4 to 5 minutes or until the lamb is cooked medium rare.

■ Remove the rack from the grill and let it rest for 10 minutes before carving into individual servings (2 ribs per person). The lamb is very good with Nan's Pan-Fried Tomatoes (see recipe, page 104).

To serve 4

8-rib rack of lamb

¼ cup olive oil

¼ cup lemon juice

1½ teaspoons honey

1 teaspoon garlic, minced

½ teaspoon Dijon mustard

¼ teaspoon cayenne pepper

Dash Worcestershire sauce

Salt to taste

■ *A CHRISTMAS MEDLEY*

Oysters with Shallot and Cilantro Butter (page 90).

Field Salad with Lemon Vinaigrette.

Honey-Basted Rack of Lamb (page 57).

Patricia's Slivered Corn (page 103).

Nan's Pan-Fried Tomatoes (page 104).

Cranberry and Orange Tart.

To serve 8

1 kid, dressed, about 8 pounds

Extra-virgin olive oil

1½ tablespoons garlic, finely chopped

1½ tablespoons cumin seeds, bruised

2 teaspoons pequín chiles, crushed

1 tablespoon salt

¾ cup extra-virgin olive oil

½ cup lime juice

■ *WHAT'S A PEQUÍN CHILE?*
Also known as the chile petin or chilequepin, this tiny, oval red pepper is scarcely larger than a baby's thumbnail. Do not be deceived by its size, because the pequín is an incendiary little bomb, especially when plucked fresh off the bush. In stores, it is usually available dried. Pequín chiles are used to flavor fresh salsas, or in dry spice rubs for beef, cabrito, or wild game.

Cabrito, or young kid, is often the highlight of outdoor celebrations in South Texas and Mexico. It is most delicious in spring when very tender, suckling kids, usually no more than 13 to 15 pounds, can be found. This classic Mexican spice rub—from Arthur and Bobbie Coleman's *The Texas Cookbook,* published in 1949 and still the best—is all the embellishment you'll need, but the cabrito is also very good served with Tart Tomatillo Salsa and warm tortillas.

■ Have your butcher quarter the kid. Two hours before you're ready to cook, rinse the kid and pat dry. Rub all over with olive oil. Combine the garlic, cumin, pequín chiles and salt and rub into the flesh. Set aside in a cool spot.

■ Build a good-sized fire of ½ mesquite wood mixed with ½ mesquite charcoal. Combine the ¾ cup olive oil and lime juice. When the coals are red-hot, but no longer flaming, put the rib sections on the grill, flesh side down. Cover and cook for 7 minutes. Turn, baste with the olive oil-lime juice mixture, and cook for 13 to 15 minutes, or until the ribs are crisp on the outside and cooked medium on the inside. Remove and set aside.

■ If necessary, replenish the coals. Put the hindquarter sections on the grill and cover. Cook for 10 to 12 minutes, flesh side down. Turn and cook, bone side down, for 13 to 15 minutes, or until the kid is cooked medium. Remove and let rest for 5 minutes.

■ To serve, carve the ribs. Cut the meat from the leg into thin slices and serve, if desired, rolled up in warm corn tortillas and topped with Tart Tomatillo Salsa (see recipe, page 118).

VENISON

VENISON FILET WITH RED WINE AND GREEN CHILES

To serve 6

1 whole venison filet, 3 to 4 pounds

2 cups dry red wine

1 carrot, thinly sliced

½ large yellow onion, thinly sliced

4 shallots, thinly sliced

2 serrano chiles, seeded and chopped

4 sprigs parsley

¼ cup extra-virgin olive oil

1 teaspoon salt

8 black peppercorns, crushed

There are two schools of venison eaters: those who love it cooked plain and those who can't bear it unless the gamy flavor has been removed. Old-time recipes call for soaking venison overnight in milk or in vinegar and water to lessen the strong taste. In this recipe, the filet or "backstrap," which is the tenderest and most delicately flavored part of the deer, is marinated in a classic red wine marinade spiked with fiery serrano chiles. It is guaranteed to convert even the most querulous eaters to the ranks of venison lovers.

1 Remove connective tissue and muscle fiber from the filet with a sharp knife. Combine all the other ingredients in a bowl and mix well. Put the venison in a shallow glass pan and pour the marinade over it, making sure that the filet is well coated on all sides. Marinate at cool room temperature for 3 hours, turning occasionally.

2 Build a mesquite wood fire. When the coals are red-hot and the flames are low, place the filet on the grill and cover. Cook for 18 to 20 minutes to medium rare, turning every 5 minutes.

3 When the venison is done, remove it from the grill and let it rest for 10 minutes before carving into ¼-inch slices.

VENISON STEAK WITH ANCHO CREAM SAUCE

For those who like their venison cooked plain, but don't mind a little embellishment on the side, this ancho chile sauce is just the ticket. Its rich, dusky flavor with just a hint of fire is a perfect match for wild game, but it's also very good with chicken and salmon grilled over mesquite.

1 To prepare the sauce, remove the stems and seeds from the chiles and tear them into small pieces. Put them in a bowl and pour boiling water over them. Let them soak for 15 to 20 minutes, or until very soft. Drain, but reserve the soaking liquid. Put the chiles in a blender or food processor along with a little of the liquid and purée until very smooth.

2 Sauté the onion in olive oil over medium-high heat until golden brown. Add the garlic and sauté for 30 seconds. Add the chile purée, ½ cup of the soaking liquid, cumin, cinnamon, and salt to taste. Reduce heat to medium and simmer for 15 minutes. Remove from the heat and press the mixture through a sieve or strainer, pressing on the solids with the back of a spoon. Set aside.

3 Rub the venison with olive oil and sprinkle with salt and pepper to taste.

4 Build a mesquite wood fire. When the coals are red-hot and the flames are low, put the venison on the grill and cover. Cook for 6 to 7 minutes per side to medium rare.

5 While the venison is cooking, return the chile mixture to the stove over medium heat. Stir in the heavy cream. Bring to a boil and remove immediately.

6 When the venison is done, remove it from the grill and let it rest for 5 to 10 minutes before carving into ½-inch slices. Serve with a generous spoonful of ancho chile cream sauce on the side.

To serve 4

Ancho cream sauce:

4 dried ancho chiles

2 cups boiling water

2 tablespoons extra-virgin olive oil

½ cup chopped onion

1 tablespoon minced garlic

1 teaspoon ground cumin

⅛ teaspoon ground cinnamon

½ cup heavy cream

2 pounds venison steak, in 1 piece

Extra-virgin olive oil

Salt and coarsely ground pepper

A REAL BARBECUE SECRET
There's hardly a backyard chef alive who doesn't believe that he or she has stumbled onto the ultimate secret of delicious barbecue. One says it's all in the sauce, while another's trick is using exotic woods.

The "secret" you almost never hear about is the simplest of all: Use the finest ingredients you can. Herbs from the garden, extra-virgin olive oil, free-range chickens, and game from your own ranch can turn an average outdoor meal into a memorable feast. If you stint on the raw materials, then all the barbecue "secrets" in the world won't help.

PORK AND VENISON SAUSAGE WITH CILANTRO

To serve 4

1 pound boneless pork

½ pound venison

1 teaspoon freshly ground black pepper

½ teaspoon freshly ground pequín chiles

1 teaspoon ground cumin

1½ teaspoons minced garlic

½ cup cilantro, minced

½ teaspoon salt

Lazy Sunday morning breakfasts are always a pleasure, especially when you have this fresh, spicy sausage to wake up your taste buds. Serve it with scrambled eggs, hot buttered biscuits, prickly pear jelly, and plenty of steaming coffee.

1 Cut the pork and venison into several pieces. Put them through the medium blade of a meat grinder twice. Put the meat in a bowl and mix it together very well.

2 Combine the herbs and spices in another bowl and mix well. If you prefer your sausage mildly flavored, begin by adding half of the ingredients to the meat mixture. Cook a little of the mixture in a frying pan and taste it for the seasonings. Keep adding seasonings and tasting it until you reach the combination you like best. Shape the sausage into patties ½ inch thick and set aside.

3 Put 1 cup of mesquite wood chips in water to soak, if desired. Build a mesquite wood fire. When the coals are red-hot and the flames are low, scatter the chips over the coals. Oil the inside of a cast-iron skillet and put the sausage patties in it. Place the skillet on the grill and cover. Cook for 7 to 8 minutes, turn the patties, and cook for another 7 to 8 minutes or until the sausage is no longer pink inside. Remove from the grill and serve at once.

MacLeod's Mesquite-Smoked Venison Chili

There are as many ways to cook chili as there are cooks, but this version—contributed by Morton MacLeod, owner of Bloomfield Farms and purveyor of triple A-rated Texas mesquite—is one of the best. It combines venison cooked over a mesquite fire with a medley of seasonings, including two kinds of chiles: The ancho chile adds a mellow glow, while the chipotle packs a wallop. As for the tomatoes, some say no authentic chili chef would use them—but they do add a pleasantly brassy note to the mix.

As with all good chili, this recipe tastes even better the day after it is made. Serve it on a gray, chilly afternoon with crusty sourdough bread and a good red wine and let its fire warm your bones.

1 Cut the venison into strips about ¾ inch thick. Rub the strips with plenty of olive oil and set aside.

2 Put 2 cups of mesquite chips in water to soak. Build a fire of ½ mesquite wood and ½ mesquite charcoal. When the coals are medium-hot and covered with a gray ash, move them to one side of the grill and cover them with wet mesquite chips. Place the venison on the grill away from the coals and cover. Cook the meat very slowly for about 30 minutes, or until it is medium, so that the meat absorbs as much of the smoke as possible without drying out. If the coals begin to fade, add

Continued on next page

To serve 4

3 pounds venison

Extra-virgin olive oil

12 dried ancho chiles

1 dried chipotle chile

½ head of garlic, peeled

**1 large yellow onion,
peeled and quartered**

4 cups water

1 tablespoon ground cumin

1 cup canned crushed tomatoes

½ teaspoon dried oregano

Salt to taste

¼ cup cilantro, minced

FAMOUS (ALLEGED) LAST WORDS
"Wish I had time for just one more bowl of chili."
—Kit Carson

a few pieces of fresh charcoal to the edges of the fire. When the venison is done, remove it from the grill and set it aside.

3 Remove the stems and seeds from the ancho and chipotle chiles and put them in separate bowls with boiling water to cover. When the ancho chiles are soft, usually after 15 to 20 minutes, drain them, but reserve the soaking liquid. Put the ancho chiles in a blender or food processor along with 1 cup of the soaking liquid and purée until very smooth. Add a little more of the liquid if necessary. Drain the chipotle chile, chop very finely, and set aside.

4 Chop the venison into bite-sized pieces. In a large stock pot, combine the meat, ancho chile mixture, cumin, oregano, tomatoes, and 4 cups of water. Let the chili simmer over medium heat, partly covered, for 1½ hours or until the meat is very tender. If the chili becomes too thick, add a little more water. After an hour, taste for seasonings. Add salt, if desired, and chipotle chile to taste.

5 Serve the chili in individual earthenware bowls, sprinkled with a little chopped cilantro.

FOWL

Chicken grilled over mesquite coals is as delicious a dish as there is, but too often the bird arrives at the table charred on the outside, raw in the center, or unpleasantly dry. Here are a few tips that will help you turn out juicy chicken—and other fowl—with wonderfully crisp skin.

1 Cut whole chickens and ducks into halves or quarters. Remove the backbone so the breast will lie flatter. To keep the skin from burning, grill over a drip pan with moderately hot coals on either side.

2 Butterfly smaller birds, such as squab, poussin, or quail by removing the backbone, opening up the bird on a flat surface, and pressing with the heel of your hand to crack the breast-bone. Cook directly over hot coals.

3 Boneless, skinless chicken or duck breasts will cook more evenly if they are first pounded with the flat side of a heavy cleaver until they are about ⅜ inch thick. Grill quickly over hot coals.

4 Use a flavorful marinade that contains some oil, or at mini-mum, oil the bird before putting it on the grill. Baste with oil or leftover marinade to keep the flesh moist and the skin crisp.

5 Test for doneness by pricking the thigh with a fork or skewer—the juices should run clear and yellow. Or press the flesh with your finger—it should feel firm to the touch.

CITRUS-FLAVORED CHICKEN WITH QUICK FOUR-PEPPER RELISH

Nothing says summer quite like the aroma of chicken sizzling over mesquite coals. Here, a lemon, lime, and orange marinade adds a slight tang to the bird. Chicken grilled this way is delicious served warm, or cold the next day—so consider fixing an extra bird for another meal.

▪Rinse the chicken, pat it dry, and place it in a large glass roasting pan. Combine the citrus juices, olive oil, and salt and pour over the chicken, making sure that all pieces are thoroughly coated. Cover and marinate in the refrigerator overnight, turning the pieces occasionally.

▪Prepare the Quick Four-Pepper Relish.

▪Build a fire of ⅓ mesquite wood mixed with ⅔ mesquite charcoal. When the coals are red-hot and the flames are low, divide the coals in half and push them to either side of the grill. Place an aluminum drip pan in the center. Place the chicken on the grill bone side down. Cover and cook for 40 to 45 minutes, turning every 10 minutes, or until the juices run yellow when the thigh is pricked with the tines of a fork.

▪Remove the chicken from the grill and let it rest for 5 or 6 minutes. Serve garnished with thin slices of lime and Quick Four-Pepper Relish.

To serve 4

2 chickens, 3 pounds each, cut in half and backbones removed

1 cup lemon juice

½ cup lime juice

¼ cup orange juice

¼ cup extra-virgin olive oil

Salt

Quick Four-Pepper Relish (see recipe, page 122)

▪*"Poultry is for the cook what canvas is for the painter."*
—Jean Anthelme Brillat-Savarin

SUMO CHICKEN WITH SCALLIONS AND SHIITAKE MUSHROOMS

To serve 4 as an appetizer
or 2 as a main course

½ pound boneless, skinless
chicken breasts

8 fresh, medium-size shiitake
mushrooms

8 scallions

6 tablespoons soy sauce

4 tablespoons sake wine

2 tablespoons safflower oil

1 tablespoon dark sesame oil

1 tablespoon grated garlic

1 tablespoon grated fresh ginger

This dish was inspired, ever so slightly, by a recipe for Japanese fried chicken given to me by a sumo wrestler turned sushi chef. While mesquite hasn't yet found its way to Japan, the seasonings of the recipe—soy, sesame, ginger, and garlic—blend beautifully with the mild aroma of an oak and mesquite wood fire. Sumo chicken is delicious served with earthy-tasting shiitake mushrooms and charred scallions.

1 Prepare the chicken by cutting it into bite-sized pieces, about 1 inch square. Remove the stems from the mushrooms and wipe the caps clean with a damp cloth. Trim the roots and tops of the scallions.

2 Combine the rest of the ingredients and pour the marinade over the chicken and mushrooms in a deep glass bowl. Marinate at cool room temperature for 45 minutes. Thread the chicken and mushrooms onto metal skewers.

3 Build a fire of ½ mesquite wood and ½ oak wood. When the coals are red-hot and covered with white ash, place the skewers and the scallions on the grill. Cover and cook for 3 minutes. Turn, cover, and cook for another 3 minutes.

4 Remove the skewered chicken and mushrooms and serve immediately with charred scallions on the side.

CHICKEN BREASTS IN CUMIN AND CAYENNE WITH PIQUE

Chicken breasts lightly marinated in olive oil, cumin, pepper, and thyme are a wonderful and blessedly simple summer Sunday supper dish. They are especially tasty when served with pique, a Columbian-style salsa mixed with chunks of ripe avocado.

1. Mix the olive oil with cumin, thyme, pepper, cayenne, and salt ahead of time so that the flavors can mingle.

2. Prepare Lucy's Pique. Stir in the avocado and refrigerate.

3. Place the chicken breasts between two sheets of wax paper on a flat surface. Pound with the flat side of a heavy meat cleaver until each breast is approximately ⅜ inch thick. Put the chicken in a shallow glass pan and coat each piece thoroughly with the olive oil mixture. Let the chicken marinate at cool room temperature for an hour.

4. Build a mesquite wood fire. When the coals are red-hot and covered with white ash, place the chicken breasts on the grill. Cover and cook for 3 minutes on each side.

5. Remove and serve immediately with a bowl of Lucy's Pique on the side.

To serve 4

3 tablespoons extra-virgin olive oil

1½ teaspoons ground cumin

1 teaspoon fresh thyme, finely chopped

½ teaspoon black pepper

¼ teaspoon cayenne

¼ teaspoon salt

Lucy's Pique (see recipe, page 117)

1 ripe avocado, peeled and mashed

2 boneless chicken breasts, halved

THE PACIFIC RIM

Sumo Chicken with Scallions and Shiitake Mushrooms (page 68).

Thinly Sliced Cucumbers in Rice Wine Vinegar.

Tuna with Soy and Wasabi (page 88).

Oriental Eggplant with Miso Sauce (page 99).

Ginger Ice Cream.

CHICKEN LIVERS WITH FRESH MORELS

To serve 4

1 pound chicken livers

¼ cup of walnut oil

2 tablespoons extra-virgin olive oil

1½ teaspoons Dijon mustard

1 tablespoon balsamic vinegar

1 teaspoon crushed pink peppercorns

Salt

¼ pound fresh morels

¼ cup extra-virgin olive oil

This unlikely pairing, quickly grilled over mesquite wood, is—to paraphrase John Lyly—"a marriage made in heaven and consumed on earth." Try this delicacy early in May when fresh morels appear in the markets.

1 Remove any fat or skin clinging to the chicken livers. If they are very large, cut them in half. Remove the stems from the morels and wipe the caps with a damp cloth.

2 Combine the walnut oil, 2 tablespoons olive oil, mustard, vinegar, peppercorns, and salt in a large glass bowl and whisk until thoroughly blended. Add the chicken livers and toss to coat. Marinate at cool room temperature for 1½ to 2 hours.

3 Build a fire of mesquite wood. While it is burning, dip the morels into the ¼ cup olive oil and thread them onto four skewers. Remove the chicken livers from the marinade and thread them onto four more skewers.

4 When the coals are red-hot and the flames have died down, place the livers on the grill, cover, and cook for 3 minutes per side. Place the morels slightly to the edge of the coals and cook for 1 to 2 minutes per side. Remove and serve 1 skewer of livers and 1 skewer of morels to each person.

POUSSIN WITH ANCHO CHILE BUTTER

Poussins are free-range baby chickens that have been fed a chemical-free diet of natural grains such as barley and rye. Far tastier than their larger cousins, poussins are splendid when very simply grilled over mesquite with a little of this mellow ancho chile butter rubbed under their skins.

1 To make the flavored butter, remove the stems and seeds from the dried chiles. Soak them in very hot water for 10 to 15 minutes, until they are soft. Put them in bowl of a blender or a food processor along with 1 or 2 tablespoons of the soaking liquid and purée.

2 Cream the butter with a fork until it is very smooth. Beat in the puréed chiles, cumin, garlic, and thyme. Add the orange juice, a tablespoon at a time, and beat well to absorb the liquid. Let the butter sit in a cool place for at least an hour so that the flavors can mingle.

3 Prepare each poussin by cutting down the backbone with a sharp knife or kitchen shears. Discard the bone or reserve for stock. Place the bird bone side down on a hard surface and

Continued on next page

To serve 4

Ancho chile butter:

  2 small dried ancho chiles

  8 ounces sweet butter, softened

  ½ teaspoon ground cumin

  ¼ teaspoon garlic

  ¼ teaspoon thyme

  3 tablespoons orange juice

4 poussins, about 1 pound each

■ *THE MOREL OF THE TALE*
Morels are the most exquisite of wild mushrooms. They make a rare appearance in late spring and can be found only in four states: Washington, Oregon, Wisconsin, and Michigan. They are easily recognized by their pitted, conical caps and intoxicatingly earthy perfume. Delicious when grilled, they make a sublime accompaniment for veal chops and filet mignon. Try them, too, with their caps stuffed with fresh foie gras.

press firmly with the heel of your hand to crack the breast-bone. Gently loosen the skin over the breast and thighs, taking care not to tear it, and insert some of the butter between the skin and flesh. Save a little butter to rub on the outside of the skin.

Build a fire of ½ mesquite wood and ½ oak wood. When the coals are red-hot and the flames are low, place the poussins on the grill, bone side down. Cover and cook for 8 minutes per side. Turn and cook for a final 5 to 7 minutes, or until the juices run yellow when the thigh is pricked with the tines of a fork.

Let the poussins rest for 5 or 6 minutes before serving. Excellent served with Patricia's Slivered Corn (see recipe, page 103).

SQUAB WITH ROSEMARY AND BLACK OLIVES

In Florence, on one of the crooked little streets that run off the Duomo, there is a wonderful, half-hidden restaurant where succulent pigeons are grilled over an open fire of olive, oak, and other woods. These delectable birds, which are simply rubbed with oil, garlic, and rosemary, are equally good when grilled over a mesquite and oak fire.

1 Prepare the squab by cutting down the backbone with a sharp knife or kitchen shears. Discard the bone or reserve for stock. Place each squab bone side down on a hard surface and crack the breastbone by pressing firmly with the heel of your hand.

2 Rub the birds all over with olive oil and sprinkle with salt and pepper. Finely chop 4 sprigs of fresh rosemary and the cloves of garlic and strew them over the birds. Set them aside in a cool place for an hour or so.

3 Build a fire of ½ mesquite wood and ½ oak wood. When the coals are red-hot and the flames are very low, place the squab on the grill and cover. Cook for about 8 minutes per side to medium rare, or until the birds are lightly browned and the juices run slightly pink when the thigh is pricked with the tines of a fork.

4 To serve, arrange the squab on a large platter and strew them with niçoise olives and fresh sprigs of rosemary.

To serve 4

4 fresh squab, 1 pound each

Extra-virgin olive oil

Salt and freshly ground black pepper

4 sprigs fresh rosemary

4 cloves garlic

12 niçoise olives

6 sprigs fresh rosemary

■ *WHY MESQUITE CHARCOAL IS BEST*
The secret of mesquite charcoal is that it is made only of heartwood, the dense inner core of the mesquite log. This yields a very pure, long-burning charcoal that produces a high, even heat.

Other types of charcoal, such as hickory, are made of "slash," the bark and other waste material that is removed when logs are milled. This kind of charcoal is aromatic but very brittle, and it burns up quickly, often before food is completely cooked.

To serve 4

8 quail

¼ cup mesquite honey

2 tablespoons dry red wine

2 tablespoons red wine vinegar

2 tablespoons olive oil

4 yellow squash

2 tablespoons melted butter

Salt and coarsely ground pepper to taste

One of the most pleasant vacilandos, or meanderings, one can take in the brush country is the search for the rare beekeeper who has mesquite honey for sale. It is usually harvested early in the summer after the trees have burst into greenish-yellow blossoms exuding a sweet nectar that sends bees into ecstacy. The deep golden honey has a subtle flavor that perfectly complements quail and other wild game, such as venison.

1 Prepare the quail by cutting down the backbone with a sharp knife or kitchen shears. Discard the bone or reserve for stock. Place each quail bone side down on a hard surface and crack the breastbone by pressing firmly with the heel of the hand. Put the birds on a platter and set aside.

2 Combine the honey, red wine, vinegar, and olive oil in a small bowl and mix well. Brush a little of the mixture over the birds. Cut the squash in half and brush with melted butter.

3 Build a mesquite wood fire. When the coals are red-hot, but no longer flaming, place the quail on the grill bone side down and cover. Cook for 4 minutes, baste with the honey mixture, turn, and cook for another 4 minutes. Baste again, turn, and cook for 2 to 3 minutes longer or until the juices run clear when the thigh is pricked with the tines of a fork. Grill the squash 3 to 4 minutes per side, or until soft and slightly brown.

4 Serve each person 2 quail, sprinkled with salt and pepper to taste, and 2 halves of the grilled squash.

QUAIL IN LIME AND TEQUILA

This unusual marinade, spiked with incendiary pequín chiles, enhances the dark, flavorful meat of the quail.

1 Prepare the quail by cutting down the backbone with a sharp knife or kitchen shears. Discard the bone or reserve for stock. Place each quail, bone side down, on a hard surface and crack the breastbone by pressing firmly with the heel of the hand.

2 Combine the tequila, lime juice, and 2 tablespoons safflower oil in a small bowl and mix well. Place the quail in a shallow glass pan and pour the marinade over them, making sure that they are coated on all sides. Crush the pequín chiles and rub them into the skin of the birds. Bruise the thyme leaves slightly and sprinkle over the quail. Let the birds stand at cool room temperature for 1½ hours, turning occasionally.

3 Build a mesquite wood fire. Remove the quail from the marinade, rub them with 1 tablespoon of safflower oil, and sprinkle with salt and pepper to taste. When the coals are red-hot, but no longer flaming, place the quail on the grill, bone side down, and cover. Cook for 4 minutes, turn, and cook for another 4 minutes. Turn again and cook for 2 to 3 minutes, or until the breast meat is still slightly pink, but the thigh juices run clear and yellow when pricked with the tines of a fork.

4 Remove the quail from the grill. Peel the avocado and cut into 8 slices. Serve each person 2 quail garnished with 2 slices of avocado.

To serve 4

8 quail

½ cup tequila

¼ cup lime juice

2 tablespoons safflower oil

4 sprigs fresh thyme

4 pequín chiles

1 tablespoon safflower oil

1 firm, ripe avocado

DRUNKEN WILD GAME DINNER
Quail in Lime and Tequila (page 75).
Mallard Duck Basted with Cognac and Ginger (page 78).
Lucy's Corncakes (page 128).
Venison Filet with Red Wine and Green Chiles (page 60).
Salad of Bitter Greens with Mustard Vinaigrette.
Maple-Bourbon Soufflé.
Black Coffee.

PHEASANT WITH VODKA AND RED PEPPER

To serve 4

4 pheasants, 1 pound each

4 slices fresh pork fat, about ⅛ inch thick

2 tablespoons walnut oil

4 tablespoons vodka

1 teaspoon cayenne pepper

1 tablespoon slivered lemon zest

Pheasant is delicious when simply marinated in a little walnut oil, red pepper, and vodka and grilled over a mesquite wood fire. To keep the breast meat moist and juicy, slip a thin piece of fresh pork fat between the skin and the breast.

1 Prepare each pheasant by cutting down the backbone with a sharp knife or kitchen shears. Discard the bone, or reserve for stock. Place the pheasant bone side down on a hard surface and crack the breastbone by pressing firmly with the heel of your hand. Tuck the wing tips behind the wing joint. Carefully loosen the skin over the breast and slip a piece of pork fat underneath it.

2 Rub the pheasants all over with walnut oil and sprinkle with vodka, cayenne, and lemon zest on both sides. Let the birds marinate at cool room temperature for 1 hour.

3 Build a mesquite wood fire. When the coals are red-hot and no longer flaming, place the pheasants on the grill bone side down. Cover and cook for 7 to 8 minutes. Turn and cook for another 7 to 8 minutes, or until the leg joint moves easily and juices run yellow when the thigh is pricked with a fork.

4 Remove the birds from the grill, let them rest for 5 minutes, and serve. Acorn Squash with Maple Butter (see recipe, page 105) is a good accompaniment.

DUCK BREASTS IN RED WINE WITH JUNIPER BERRIES

1 Place each duck breast between 2 sheets of wax paper and pound with the flat side of a heavy cleaver until the breast meat is about ⅜ inch thick. Place the duck in a shallow glass pan.

2 Combine the wine, 2 tablespoons olive oil, juniper berries, peppercorns, coriander seeds, shallots, and garlic. Pour marinade over the duck breasts and marinate for 2 to 3 hours at cool room temperature, or 4 to 6 hours in the refrigerator, turning every hour or so.

3 Build a mesquite wood fire. While it is burning, remove the breasts from the marinade. Rub them all over with 1 tablespoon of olive oil and sprinkle with salt and pepper to taste.

4 When the coals are red-hot and the flames have died down, place the duck breasts on the grill and cover. Cook for 3 minutes on each side, or just until the breasts are slightly pink in the center.

5 Serve duck breasts accompanied by a generous spoonful of coarse-grained mustard and Wild Mushroom Scramble (see recipe, page 111).

To serve 4

4 duck breasts, ½ pound each, skinned and boned

1 cup dry red wine

2 tablespoons extra-virgin olive oil

4 juniper berries, crushed

8 black peppercorns, crushed

¼ teaspoon coriander seeds, crushed

2 tablespoons minced shallots

1 large clove garlic, peeled and crushed

1 tablespoon extra-virgin olive oil

Salt and freshly ground pepper

TASTES OF AUTUMN
Duck Breasts in Red Wine with Juniper Berries (page 77).
Wild Mushroom Scramble (page 111).
Chestnut Purée.
Salad of Pear and Radicchio.
Baked Apples with Heavy Cream.

MALLARD DUCK BASTED WITH COGNAC AND GINGER

To serve 2

1 mallard duck, about 2 pounds

1½ tablespoons extra-virgin olive oil

1 teaspoon fresh rosemary, minced

Coarse salt and freshly ground black pepper

Juice of 1 lime

⅓ cup cognac

2 tablespoons honey

1 tablespoon fresh ginger, peeled and chopped

1 tablespoon olive oil

Wild mallard ducks have darker, leaner, and more flavorful meat than their pen-raised brethren. Their slight gaminess is nicely set off by this mellow cognac, ginger, and honey glaze and the aroma of a mesquite fire. The glaze can also be used with Long Island and other domestic ducklings.

1 Using a sharp heavy knife, split the duck in half. Discard the giblets or reserve for another use. Rinse well and pat dry. Rub the duck all over with olive oil, rosemary, coarse salt, and black pepper. Squeeze the juice of 1 lime over the duck and set aside in a cool place for 2 hours.

2 Combine the cognac, honey, ginger, and 1 tablespoon olive oil in a small, nonaluminum saucepan. Simmer gently for 4 to 5 minutes until the mixture just begins to thicken. Remove from heat and let cool to room temperature.

3 Build a fire of ½ mesquite charcoal and ½ mesquite wood. When the coals are red-hot, but no longer flaming, place the duck halves bone side down on the grill. Cover and cook for 30 minutes, turning every 10 minutes. Brush the duck all over with the cognac-ginger glaze; cover and cook for another 5 minutes. Brush with the glaze again, turn, and cook for a final 5 minutes or until the juices run yellow when the thigh is pricked with the tines of a fork.

4 Remove the duck from the grill and let it rest for 5 minutes. Serve garnished with fresh watercress and a generous spoonful of Pat's Louisiana Peach Chutney (see recipe, page 124).

WILD TURKEY WITH WILD RICE, SCALLION, AND PECAN DRESSING

The wild turkey is the wiliest of game birds—or so the story goes. Even the most patient hunters have given up in frustration after a day in a cold, damp blind waiting for this elusive prey to make an appearance—and all the while the sly creature may be lurking just yards away in a creek bottom. The turkey's "invisibility" has led to many a tall tale, such as the one about the crafty gobbler who tracked his hunters by following in their own footsteps.

But if you are lucky enough to bag this prince of birds—even if it's a corn-fed one from the butcher—you will find that it makes splendid eating. Built for running and flying, the wild turkey has darker meat and lacks the thick, tasteless breast of its commercially bred cousins. Best are the young hens, especially if their tender flesh happens to be flavored with the peppery taste of pequín chiles pecked from bushes growing in the wild.

To cook a wild turkey over mesquite, you must have a covered grill large enough to accommodate the bird's high, arched breastbone. Otherwise, consider splitting the turkey in half and cooking it, bone side down, over the coals. Either way, the grill must be covered, since the bird is really being roasted over a charcoal fire. Served with a buttery wild rice and pecan dressing, a wild turkey is a wonderful centerpiece for a very special Thanksgiving or Christmas dinner.

1 Put 2 cups of mesquite chips in water to soak.

2 Rinse the turkey with cool water and pat dry. Reserve the neck and giblets for another use. Rub the turkey inside and out with olive oil and sprinkle with salt and pepper to taste. Peel the shallots, cut them in half, and place them in the cavity of the turkey along with the fresh sage. Tuck the wings behind the back and tie the legs together with a piece of twine. Sprinkle the bird all over with a little dry vermouth.

3 Build a good-sized fire of mesquite charcoal. When the coals are red-hot and the flames have died down, divide the

Continued on next page

To serve 6

1 wild turkey, about 8 pounds

2 tablespoons extra-virgin olive oil

Salt and freshly ground pepper

4 shallots

2 sprigs fresh sage

1 tablespoon dry vermouth

Dressing:

¾ cup shelled pecans

1 cup wild rice

1½ cups boiling water

1 tablespoon butter

¾ cup scallions, chopped

Salt and freshly ground pepper

PILGRIM'S PROGRESS
Wild Turkey with Wild Rice, Scallion, and Pecan Dressing (page 79).
Acorn Squash with Maple Butter (page 105).
Orange, Jicama, and Red Onion Salad.
Individual Pecan Tarts.

coals in half and push them to opposite sides of the grill. Place an aluminum drip pan in the center. Place the turkey, breast side up, on the grill directly over the drip pan and cover. Cook for 11 to 12 minutes per pound, or until a meat thermometer registers 185°F when it is inserted in the thickest part of the thigh.

After 45 minutes or so, check the fire to see if the coals need replenishing. If so, add a few pieces of charcoal to the edges of the hot coals. Thirty minutes before the turkey is done, add the wet mesquite chips to the coals for a smokier mesquite flavor.

If at any time it seems as though the turkey is browning too quickly, make a "hat" out of aluminum foil and cover the bird loosely.

4 While the turkey is cooking, prepare the dressing: Preheat the oven to 300°F. Put the pecans in a shallow baking pan and place them on the top rack of the oven. Toast for 4 to 5 minutes, turn with a spatula, and cook for another 4 to 5 minutes, or until the pecans are nicely crisp. (Watch carefully so that they do not burn.) Remove the pecans from the oven, let them cool, and chop into small pieces.

5 About an hour before the turkey is done, start the wild rice. Put the rice in a large sieve or strainer and rinse under cold running water for 2 minutes. Bring water in the bottom of a double boiler to a boil. Put the rice, 1½ cups boiling water, 1 tablespoon butter, and salt and pepper in the top of the double boiler and cover. Lower the heat and cook the rice over simmering water for 55 minutes, or until it is tender.

6 When the turkey is done, remove it from the grill. Reserve the juices in the drip pan. Sauté the scallions in 2 tablespoons butter. When the rice is ready, stir the scallions and chopped pecans into the rice. Add pan drippings to taste.

7 Carve the turkey and serve with wild rice dressing on the side.

FISH AND SHELLFISH

There are nearly as many ways to cook fish outdoors as there are fish in the sea. Here are a few simple pointers:

1. Always begin with an impeccably clean grill. Oil it and let it heat up over the coals before you put the fish on top.

2. Fish steaks—say, of salmon, tuna, or swordfish—should be cut ¾ to 1 inch thick. Marinate or rub with oil and grill over hot coals. (If the fire is too cool, the fish will taste "wet" and mushy.)

3. Grill fish fillets with the skin on—slash them to keep them from puckering. Or wrap them in packets of banana leaves or aluminum foil to gently steam them. Add a few sprigs of fresh herbs, lemon slices, and butter for extra flavor.

4. Whole large fish are best cooked in a hinged grilling basket. Smaller fish, such as trout or baby salmon, can be cooked directly on the grill. Turn them with a large flat spatula to keep them from falling apart.

5. Although the standard rule is to grill fish for 10 minutes per inch of flesh, you may find that mesquite's hotter fire reduces the required cooking time. Fish is done when the flesh is opaque and the skin pulls away from the flesh—if you wait until it flakes, it's probably overdone.

COLETTE'S "KICKED FISH"

In *Prisons et Paradis,* the French author Colette writes sensuously of a fish grilled in a forest of southern Provence. The fire was built of "twisted olive logs, bundles of cistus, laurel roots . . . a scant gathering of terebinth, almond, and of course a few vine-cuttings." The fish were Mediterranean—"an ugly rockfish . . . with a dragon mouth; or a few thin dark-backed mullets"—and they were brushed with a "broom" of laurel, mint, thyme, rosemary, and sage dunked in good olive oil, pink vinegar, and garlic "pounded to the consistency of cream."

The wood was burned to a thick bed of embers, and then, just before the fish was placed on the grill, the fire was given "an authoritative kick, one that sends sparks and smoke and embers flying, that exposes the burning pink coals, levels them, uncovering the pure heart of the fire, above which hovers a tiny blue flame, a wisp of fiery ghost. . . ."

"The 'kicked' fish leaps from the grill onto your plate. You see how firm it is, how its skin crackles, splits, and reveals the white flesh whose taste recalls the ocean and the odor of the forest. The pine-scented night begins to fall, and a flickering candle on the table illuminates the pomegranate color of the wine in your glass. The moment is full of happiness. Drink to it."

Need one say more? Here is a version of Colette's recipe, with ingredients more readily found in America: baby salmon for the fish and a mixture of hickory, oak, and mesquite for the wood. If you can't find baby salmon in your fish market, the recipe is nearly as good with trout.

1 Rinse the salmon and pat dry inside and out.

2 With a mortar and pestle, mash the garlic until it is soft and

Continued on next page

To serve 4

4 whole baby salmon, cleaned, ¾ pound each

2 large cloves garlic

⅓ cup extra-virgin olive oil

3 tablespoons balsamic vinegar

½ teaspoon freshly ground black pepper

Salt

2 sprigs fresh rosemary

2 sprigs fresh thyme

2 sprigs fresh mint

2 sprigs fresh sage

4 slices bacon

■ *HOW TO COOK FISH*
No cheese, no nonsense! Just place it tenderly in fig leaves and tie them on top with a string; then push it under hot ashes, bethinking thee wisely of the time when it is done, and burn it not up.
—*Archestratus,* Gastrology, *4th Century B.C.*

creamy. Combine the oil and vinegar in a small bowl. Add the garlic, salt, and pepper and mix well.

Gather the herbs together and tie the stems with a piece of kitchen string. Dip the "broom" in the oil and vinegar mixture and brush it all over the fish, inside and out. Stuff each fish with a piece of bacon and set aside in a cool place.

Build a fire of mesquite charcoal mixed with a few chunks of hickory and oak. When the coals are red-hot, but no longer flaming, brush the fish again with the oil and vinegar mixture and put them on the grill. Give the grill a sharp rap with a pair of tongs (or a gentle kick with your foot) to fire the coals and cover. Cook for 5 minutes. Brush the fish on both sides with the oil and vinegar mixture; turn and cook for 4 to 5 minutes longer. The fish are done when the pale pink flesh is opaque and the skin is crisped to a deep golden brown.

SWORDFISH WITH ROSEMARY AND LIME BUTTER

Thick, meaty swordfish steaks are wonderful when grilled over hot mesquite coals. They need no embellishment other than a flavorful compound butter, such as this rosemary and lime combination.

■ Cream the butter with a fork until it is very smooth. Beat in the lemon and lime juice. Add the garlic and rosemary and mix well. Set aside for at least an hour in a cool spot so that the flavors can mingle.

■ Rub the swordfish with olive oil on all sides and sprinkle with salt and pepper to taste.

■ Build a fire of ½ mesquite wood and ½ mesquite charcoal. When the flames are low but still licking over red-hot coals, place the fish on the grill and cover. Cook for 4 to 5 minutes per side, or until the fish is cooked through.

■ When the fish is done, remove it from the grill. Serve with a generous spoonful of the rosemary-lime butter on top of each steak.

To serve 4

Rosemary-lime butter:

4 ounces sweet butter, softened

1 tablespoon lemon juice

2 teaspoons lime juice

1 large clove garlic, minced

2 teaspoons fresh rosemary, minced

4 swordfish steaks, 1 inch thick

Extra-virgin olive oil

Salt and freshly ground black pepper

■ *IN WESTERN TEXAS
the prairies and oak-openings—
the mesquit bush
pecan tree
and prickly pear;
and the far-stretching spread of the
land carpeted with
flowers*

—Walt Whitman.

SWORDFISH WITH EGGPLANT AND SWEET RED PEPPERS

To serve 4

½ cup extra-virgin olive oil

¼ cup lemon juice

2 tablespoons lime juice

3 cloves garlic, minced

1 tablespoon grated
lemon zest

4 to 5 sprigs fresh parsley,
chopped

3 to 4 sprigs fresh rosemary,
chopped

Salt and freshly ground pepper

2½ pounds swordfish steaks
or "bits"

3 oriental eggplants

2 large sweet red peppers

Extra-virgin olive oil

Swordfish is especially succulent when marinated in olive oil, lemon juice, and fresh herbs before grilling. If you are lucky enough to vacation in Nantucket or Martha's Vineyard, this recipe is a good way to use the swordfish "bits" or trimmings that are sold in the fish markets there.

In a glass bowl, whisk the olive oil, lemon juice, and lime juice together. Add the garlic, lemon zest, fresh herbs, and salt and pepper to taste. Trim the swordfish and cut it into 1-inch cubes. Place the fish in a shallow glass pan and pour the marinade over it, making sure that all pieces are thoroughly coated. Marinate in the refrigerator for at least 2 hours, turning occasionally.

Trim the ends of the eggplants and slice into rounds 1 inch thick. Remove the stems and seeds from the red pepper and cut into 1½ inch chunks. Brush both with olive oil and set aside.

Build a fire of ½ mesquite wood and ½ mesquite charcoal. Remove the swordfish from the marinade and thread onto 4 long skewers. Thread the vegetables onto 4 more skewers. When the flames are low and the coals are red-hot, place the skewers on the grill and cover. Cook for 4 to 5 minutes per side, or until the swordfish is cooked through. Be careful not to overcook.

When ready, remove the skewers from the grill and serve each guest a skewer of fish and a skewer of vegetables, garnished with slices of lime and fresh rosemary, if desired.

RED SNAPPER GRILLED IN BANANA LEAVES

Banana leaves are often used in southern climes to keep food moist as it is cooked. In this recipe, red snapper fillets are lightly seasoned with cilantro, ginger, and lemon grass and wrapped up in a fresh banana leaf before being grilled over mesquite charcoal. When the packets are opened, the fish emerges beautifully tender and with an exquisite aroma.

■ Prepare the banana leaves: Using a sharp knife, split the leaves down the back and remove the central spine. Pass them over a medium-hot flame or burner until they are wilted and very soft. Wipe clean with a sponge and pat dry. Brush the leaves generously on both sides with safflower oil.

■ Rub the skin side of the red snapper fillets with a few drops of oil and sprinkle with salt and pepper to taste. Lay one banana leaf on a flat surface and place one fillet on top of it. Place a sprig of cilantro, a few ginger matchsticks, and a couple of pieces of lemon grass on top. (Don't overdo it, use just a little of each for flavor.) Wrap the banana leaf around the filet, just as you would wrap a gift package. Tie with two thin strips of banana leaf or a length of kitchen twine, to keep the packet closed.

■ Build a fire of mesquite charcoal. When the coals are red-hot and the flames are low, place the banana leaf packets on the grill and cover. Cook for 7 to 8 minutes without turning. Unwrap and serve at once with a little butter and a sprinkle of lime juice.

To serve 6

6 red snapper fillets, ½ pound each

3 to 4 large fresh banana leaves (available at some Asian and Latin American markets)

Safflower oil

Salt and freshly ground pepper

6 sprigs cilantro

1 piece fresh ginger, peeled and cut into matchsticks

2 stalks lemon grass, cut into 1-inch pieces and crushed slightly

■ *A GRAZING PARTY*

Miniature Hamburgers with Chunky Guacamole (page 36).

Sliced Filet Stuffed with Sun-Dried Tomatoes, Pine Nuts, and Capers (page 35).

Chicken Livers with Fresh Morels (page 70).

Swordfish with Eggplant and Red Peppers (page 86).

Hawaiian Prawns with Scallions and Shiitake Mushrooms (page 93).

Baby Back Ribs with Bourbon-Honey Glaze (page 47).

Barbecued Pork Tacos with Two Lively Sauces (page 45).

(This is finger food. The normal yield for each recipe can be doubled by serving smaller portions.)

TUNA WITH SOY AND WASABI

To serve 4

4 tuna steaks, ¾ inch thick

2 tablespoons safflower oil

Salt and freshly ground pepper

2 tablespoons dry wasabi (Japanese horseradish)

2 tablespoons water

¼ cup soy sauce

¼ cup lemon juice

2 tablespoons grated ginger

¼ cup minced scallions

Fresh tuna is delicious when grilled just to medium rare inside. Try it with a dipping sauce of soy and lemon and a dab of wasabi, the pungent pale-green Japanese horseradish that is usually served with sushi and sashimi.

1 Rub the tuna steaks with safflower oil, sprinkle with salt and pepper to taste, and set aside.

2 In a small bowl, mix the wasabi and water together until they form a smooth paste. Turn the bowl upside down (the wasabi will stick to the inside) and set aside until ready to use.

3 Mix the soy sauce and lemon juice in another bowl and set aside.

4 Build a fire of mesquite charcoal mixed with a few chunks of mesquite wood. When the flames are low and the coals are red-hot, put the fish on the grill and cover. Cook for 3 minutes per side to medium rare, or 2 minutes longer if you prefer your tuna well done.

5 Serve the fish with individual bowls of soy and lemon for dipping, along with small dishes of wasabi, grated ginger, and scallions. Let each guest use chopsticks to mix the wasabi, ginger, and scallions into his or her sauce to taste.

SALMON WITH PINK AND WHITE PEPPERCORNS

Salmon is a rich, oily fish whose flavor is enhanced by the fragrance of a mesquite fire and the mildly aromatic scent of pink and white peppercorns.

1 Coarsely grind the peppercorns in a spice mill, or pulverize them with a mortar and pestle. Mix well.

2 Rub the salmon with safflower oil all over. Thickly sprinkle the ground peppercorns on the fish and press them into the flesh. Sprinkle with salt to taste.

3 Build a fire of ⅔ mesquite charcoal and ⅓ mesquite wood. When the flames are low and the coals are red-hot, put the fish on the grill and cover. Cook for 5 minutes per side.

4 Remove the fish from the grill and serve sizzling hot, garnished with thin slices of lime.

To serve 6

6 salmon steaks, 1 inch thick

3 tablespoons safflower oil

2 tablespoons pink peppercorns

1½ tablespoons white peppercorns

Salt

3 limes, thinly sliced

**To serve 4 as an appetizer
or 2 as a main course**

24 large oysters in their shells

¾ cup dry white wine

¼ cup shallots, minced

**8 ounces sweet butter, chilled
and cut into 8 pieces**

2 tablespoons cilantro, minced

It may have been a brave man who first ate an oyster, but when these succulent crustaceans are grilled over mesquite charcoal, the only willpower involved is in not devouring every one. This festive dish would make a wonderful appetizer for Christmas dinner, or a splendid main course for 2.

1 Scrub the oysters well under cold, running water to remove the dirt and grit from their shells.

2 Combine the wine and the shallots in a nonaluminum saucepan over high heat and bring to a boil. Reduce over high heat to 3 tablespoons. Set aside.

3 Build a fire of ⅔ mesquite charcoal and ⅓ mesquite wood. When the coals are medium-hot and covered with grayish ash, place the oysters on the grill, flat side up. Cover and cook for 7 or 8 minutes, or until the shells have just opened.

4 While the oysters are cooking, place the saucepan with the wine-shallot mixture over medium-high heat. Using a wire whisk, beat in the chilled butter, piece by piece, until the mixture is smooth and creamy. Stir in the cilantro. Remove from the heat, but keep warm.

5 When the oysters are done, remove them from the grill. Using a knife, open the oysters and remove the top shell. Spoon a little of the butter sauce over each oyster and serve at once.

LOBSTER WITH TOMATO AND RED PEPPER SAUCE

This splendid summer dish is adapted from Elizabeth David's recipe for Lobster Romesco, which appears in *A Book of Mediterranean Food.* The smooth but intensely flavored sauce is also good with mesquite-grilled fish.

1 Put a large pot of water on to boil.

2 Build a fire of mesquite charcoal. When the flames are high, place the tomatoes and garlic cloves on the grill at the edges of the coals so that they can soften without burning. Impale the peppers on a long-handled fork and hold them directly in the flames until the skin is blistered and blackened.

3 Put the peppers in a plastic bag or paper sack, close it tightly, and let the peppers steam for 10 minutes. When the tomatoes and garlic cloves are very soft, remove them from the grill. Peel the tomatoes, cut them in half, and squeeze out the juice. Chop the tomatoes coarsely. Peel the garlic cloves and chop coarsely. Remove the peppers from the sack and rub the skins off with your fingers. Remove the stems, seeds, and inner membranes and cut in quarters.

4 Combine the tomatoes, garlic, and peppers in a food processor or blender and purée. Stir in the olive oil, vinegar, paprika, and salt to taste. Set aside.

5 Revive the fire with fresh chunks of mesquite charcoal, if necessary. Drop the lobsters in the pot of boiling water for 1 minute. Remove, split them in half, and discard the sac near the eyes. Brush the lobster flesh with melted butter.

6 When the coals are red-hot, but no longer flaming, put the lobsters on the grill, flesh side up, and cover. Cook for 7 to 8 minutes, turn, and cook for 3 to 4 minutes more, or until the lobster meat is opaque.

7 When the lobsters are done, remove them from the grill and crack the claws. Serve with individual bowls of tomato and red pepper sauce on the side. Garnish with sprigs of fresh basil.

To serve 4

2 large ripe tomatoes

2 large sweet red peppers

4 large cloves of garlic, unpeeled

¼ cup extra-virgin olive oil

1½ teaspoons red wine vinegar

1½ teaspoons sweet paprika

4 live lobsters, 1¼ pounds each

2 tablespoons melted butter

Sprigs of fresh basil for garnish

FIRST DAY OF SPRING DINNER
Lobster with Tomato and Red Pepper Sauce (page 91).
Fresh Asparagus with Lemon Butter.
New Potatoes with Chives.
Fresh Strawberries with Heavy Cream.

To serve 6

24 medium shrimp in their shells

2 chicken breasts, boned and skinned

½ cup lemon juice

½ cup extra-virgin olive oil

½ cup finely chopped onion

¼ cup shredded basil leaves

½ cup slivered sweet red pepper

Salt

3 large sweet red peppers

6 serrano chiles

Extra-virgin olive oil

FATHER'S DAY DINNER
Lemony Shrimp and Chicken with Red and Green Peppers (page 92).
Steak with Grilled Red Onions and Poblano Chiles(page 31).
Hellzapoppin' Potato Chips (page 109).
Avocado and Tomato Salad with Cilantro.
Lemon Meringue Pie.

Shrimp and chicken make a wonderful combination when lightly marinated in lemon juice and herbs and grilled on a skewer. The sweet red pepper and hot green serrano chile intensify this medley of flavors.

1 Devein the shrimp by cutting down the back of the shell with a sharp paring knife. Rinse and pat dry. Do not remove the shells or legs.

2 Cut the chicken into bite-sized pieces about 1½ inches square.

3 Put the shrimp and chicken into separate bowls. Mix the lemon juice, olive oil, onion, basil, and ½ cup slivered red pepper together and pour half over the shrimp and half over the chicken. Toss to coat. Let both marinate at cool room temperature for 45 minutes, turning occasionally.

4 Remove the stems, seeds, and inner membranes of the red peppers and cut lengthwise into strips ¾ inch wide. Remove the stems of the green chiles. Brush with olive oil and set aside.

5 Build a fire of ½ mesquite wood and ½ mesquite charcoal. While the fire is burning, remove the shrimp and chicken from the marinade. Alternately thread the shrimp, chicken, and peppers onto the skewers. When the coals are hot, but no longer flaming, put the skewers on the grill and cover. Cook for 4 minutes per side, or until the shrimp are opaque and the chicken is no longer springy to the touch.

6 Remove from the grill and serve 2 skewers to each person, garnished with sprigs of fresh basil, if desired.

HAWAIIAN PRAWNS WITH SCALLIONS AND SHIITAKE MUSHROOMS

A couple of years ago a few West Coast restaurants began firing their grills with kiawe wood from Hawaii. Menus touted its superb aroma and long-lasting coals, and more than one critic predicted that kiawe would supplant mesquite as the grilling wood of choice.

Mesquite lovers had the last laugh, however, since kiawe is simply the Hawaiian variety of the same tree. Mesquite was brought to Hawaii around 1830, and by 1910, a Hawaii Agricultural Experiment Station Report praised it as "the most valuable tree thus far introduced into the island." During the 1920s, 500,000 bags of dry pods were picked and stored each year to use as animal feed.

Whether you use kiawe or mesquite wood, these magnificent blue prawns, marinated in fiery Szechuan spices, taste just as good as they look. They're especially delicious when wrapped in green scallions and grilled with plump shiitake mushrooms.

1 Devein the shrimp by cutting down the back of the shell with a sharp paring knife. Rinse and pat dry. Do not remove shells or legs.

2 Combine the safflower oil, dark sesame oil, chili oil, lime juice, soy sauce, ginger, Szechuan peppers, and red pepper in a large glass bowl and mix well. Trim the roots and green tops from the scallions, reserving the tops. Chop the white bulbs and add to the marinade. Add the shrimp and toss to coat with the

Continued on next page

To serve 4

16 Hawaiian prawns (or substitute jumbo shrimp), in their shells

½ cup safflower oil

2 tablespoons dark sesame oil

1 teaspoon hot chili oil

6 tablespoons lime juice

4 tablespoons soy sauce

2 tablespoons grated fresh ginger

1 tablespoon crushed Szechuan peppers

1 crushed dried red pepper

1 bunch scallions

16 fresh shiitake mushrooms

2 tablespoons safflower oil

TIPS FOR SHELLFISH
It's easy to grill lobsters, shrimp, and oysters since their protective carapaces keep them moist and tender. Here are a few simple ways to cook them over coals:

1. Plunge lobsters into boiling water for 1 minute. Cut in half, brush with oil or butter, and grill over moderately hot coals.

2. Shrimp will be succulent if marinated in oil and grilled in their shells until golden brown.

3. Oysters, clams, and mussels need only be scrubbed clean. Grill over a medium-hot fire until shells open. Serve with melted butter flavored with garlic, lemon, your favorite herbs, or roasted and pureed peppers.

mixture. Let shrimp marinate at cool room temperature for 1 hour, or in the refrigerator for 2 hours, turning occasionally.

3 Put 1 cup of mesquite chips in water to soak. Build a fire of mesquite charcoal in your grill. While it is burning, remove the stems from the shiitake mushrooms, wipe the caps with a damp cloth, and brush them all over with safflower oil. Remove the shrimp from the marinade. Wrap a green scallion top crisscross fashion around each shrimp, securing the ends as you impale the shrimp on a metal skewer. Alternate with shiitake mushrooms. Brush with a little leftover marinade.

4 When the coals are hot but no longer flaming, toss the wet mesquite chips on the coals. Place the skewers on the grill and cover. Cook for 4 to 5 minutes per side or until the shrimp are opaque and the shells are just beginning to turn golden brown.

5 Remove and serve each person two skewers of shrimp and mushrooms.

MIXED SHELLFISH WITH RED PEPPER, TARRAGON, AND GINGER BUTTERS

This sumptuous array of crustaceans, served with a trio of flavorful butter sauces, is the ultimate in gastronomic self-indulgence.

Midway through the cooking, all the shellfish will be on the grill at the same time, so be sure to start with a good-sized bed of coals. If your grill is too small to accommodate all the sea-food, or if you plan to double or triple the recipe, grill the lob-sters first. While your guests are devouring them, you can cook the rest of the shellfish and serve them as a second course.

1 Put a large pot of water on the stove to boil.

2 Combine the olive oil, lime juice, garlic, and tarragon in a bowl and set aside.

3 Scrub the clams and oysters to remove sand and grit. Devein the shrimp by cutting through the back of the shells with a sharp knife. Do not remove the shells or legs. Rinse and pat dry. Put the shrimp in the olive oil mixture to marinate for 30 minutes. Thread them onto metal skewers and set aside.

4 When the water is boiling, drop the lobster into the pot for 1 minute. Remove and place the lobster on its back on a cutting board. With a sharp heavy knife, cut the lobster in half. Remove the sac near the eyes. Brush the flesh of the lobster with the olive oil mixture.

5 Build a good-sized fire of ⅔ mesquite charcoal mixed with ⅓ mesquite wood. Impale the red pepper on a long-handled fork and hold it in the flame until the skin is blackened and

Continued on next page

To serve 2

⅓ cup extra-virgin olive oil

2 tablespoons lime juice

1 large clove garlic, slivered

1 tablespoon fresh chopped tarragon

6 clams in the shell

6 oysters in the shell

6 large shrimp

1 live lobster, 1¼ pounds

12 ounces sweet butter

1½ teaspoons fresh minced tarragon

1 tablespoon lemon juice

1 small sweet red pepper

1 large clove garlic, sliced

2 teaspoons fresh grated ginger

1 tablespoon fresh chopped scallions

blistered. Put the pepper in a plastic bag or paper sack; close tightly and let it steam for 10 minutes. Rub off the skin and remove the stem, seeds, and inner membranes. Cut the pepper into pieces and purée it in a blender or food processor.

6 Set out 3 small bowls. Put the red pepper purée and garlic in the first bowl, the ginger and scallions in the second, and the tarragon and lemon juice in the third. Melt the butter in a small saucepan and keep warm.

7 When the coals are red-hot, but no longer flaming, put the lobster on the grill, flesh side up. Cover and cook for 2 minutes. Add the oysters, flat side up, and clams to the grill. Cover and cook for 3 minutes. Add the shrimp to the grill; cover and cook for 3 minutes. Brush the lobster and shrimp with the olive oil mixture and turn. Cover and cook for 3 to 4 minutes longer. The shellfish are ready when the lobster and shrimp are opaque and the clam and oyster shells have opened.

8 Crack the lobster claws and arrange the shellfish on a large platter. Pour equal amounts of melted butter into the bowls containing the red pepper purée, ginger, and tarragon, and mix the ingredients in each bowl well. Serve with fresh asparagus.

VEGETABLES
ON AND OFF
THE GRILL

Fresh vegetables can easily be cooked on the grill alongside the main course. Here are 4 simple techniques:

1 *In the coals.* Whole ears of corn in the shuck, silks removed, are wonderful cooked right down in medium-hot mesquite coals until slightly charred. Whole or quartered new potatoes, red onions, and summer squash take on a delectably smoky flavor when cooked the same way, but they should be wrapped in aluminum foil to prevent scorching.

2 *In the flame.* Sweet peppers turn sweeter and smokier when roasted directly in the flame of a mesquite blaze—and hot peppers mellow nicely. For a sparkling summer salad, roast red, yellow, and green bell peppers over a mesquite fire until the skins are blackened. Let peppers steam in a paper sack for 5 to 10 minutes after roasting, then peel. Drizzle with extra-virgin olive oil, a little balsamic vinegar and sprinkle with fresh chopped herbs.

3 *On the grill.* Halved or sliced purple eggplant, red onion, summer squash, zucchini, wild mushrooms, and tomatoes need only light brushing with oil for quick cooking over hot coals. Large fennel stalks, potatoes, and very large leeks should be parboiled first to speed grilling time.

4 *On skewers.* Chunks of squash, eggplant, peppers, cherry tomatoes, mushroom caps, and small white onions (parboiled first) should be grilled on metal skewers. Brush with oil first and be sure to combine vegetables that need the same cooking time.

ORIENTAL EGGPLANT WITH MISO SAUCE

The slender, pale purple eggplant that is sold in Asian markets is a superb grilling vegetable. When cooked over mesquite wood, it acquires a rich, slightly sweet flavor—without the bitterness of its larger, darker purple cousins. Brushed with a simple mixture of miso and rice wine, it is an excellent accompaniment for pork, veal, chicken, and seafood of all kinds.

1 Combine the miso, sugar, and sake in a small saucepan over low heat and stir until thoroughly blended. Remove from the heat, but keep warm.

2 Trim the stems of the eggplants and slice them in half lengthwise. Brush them all over with safflower oil.

3 Build a mesquite wood fire. When the coals are red-hot and no longer flaming, place the eggplant on the grill, cut side down. Cover and cook for 3 minutes. Turn and brush the cut side with miso sauce. Cover and cook for 2 to 3 minutes more, or until the eggplant is soft and very slightly charred. Serve immediately.

To serve 4

4 small oriental eggplants

¼ cup white miso (soybean paste)

3 tablespoons plus 1 teaspoon sugar

2 tablespoons sake (rice wine)

2 tablespoons safflower oil

A SALAD SAMPLER
A fresh, colorful salad is often the only accompaniment you'll need for food cooked on the mesquite grill. Try these delicious combinations:

1. Peppery watercress and crisp slices of sweet jicama tossed with lime juice and olive oil.

2. Sliced red onion, orange, and curly endive in a raspberry vinaigrette.

3. Bitter greens, such as arugula, radicchio, and escarole, dressed with a mustard vinaigrette.

4. Thinly sliced avocado, tomatoes, and red onion, sprinkled with lime juice and cilantro.

5. Finely chopped red and green cabbage, dressed with homemade mayonnaise and vinegar.

6. Roasted red and yellow peppers, tossed with extra-virgin olive oil and garlic.

SKEWERED ONIONS, EGGPLANT, AND RED PEPPER

To serve 4 as a side dish

8 small white onions

2 oriental eggplants

2 large sweet red peppers

1 tablespoon minced chives

1 teaspoon minced rosemary

1 teaspoon minced thyme

½ cup extra-virgin olive oil

Salt and freshly ground black pepper

Sprinkled with fresh herbs, this tasty combination of sweet onions, peppers, and smoky eggplant goes especially well with lamb or fish.

1 Peel the onions. Put them in a pot with cold water to cover and bring to a boil. Reduce heat and simmer the onions for 2 to 3 minutes, or until they are just tender when pierced with a fork. Drain and set aside.

2 Cut the eggplant into 1-inch chunks. Remove the stems, seeds, and inner membranes of the red peppers and cut into 1-inch pieces.

3 Combine the olive oil, herbs, salt, and black pepper in a bowl. Add the vegetables and toss to coat them all over. Thread them onto long metal skewers in a pleasing combination and set aside.

4 Build a fire of mesquite wood or mesquite charcoal. When the coals are hot, but no longer flaming, place the vegetables on the grill and cover. Cook for 4 minutes per side, or until the vegetables are soft and very slightly charred. Serve at once.

GOLDEN-HEARTED RED PEPPERS

This is a beautiful dish, full of sweet and smoky flavors. After the peppers are grilled, they are cut open to reveal a colorful melange of corn, green peppers, tomatoes, onion, and bacon. The stuffing is based on a traditional recipe for Creole corn from the files of Edna Morrison of New Orleans.

1 Shuck the corn and cut off the stems so that each cob will stand upright on a cutting board. Using a sharp knife, cut the kernels off the cob. There should be 2 cups.

2 In a skillet, cook the corn, onion, and green pepper in butter until the vegetables are soft, about 10 minutes. Add the tomatoes, paprika, salt, and pepper and cook for 2 minutes more. Remove from the heat and let the mixture cool.

3 Fry the bacon until crisp. Drain on several layers of paper towels. Crumble and set aside.

4 Cut off the tops of the red peppers about ½ inch down from the stems. Reserve the tops. Remove the seeds and inner membranes. Mix the bacon with the corn and spoon the mixture into the red peppers. Replace the tops and secure with toothpicks or small skewers.

5 Build a mesquite wood fire. When the coals are medium-hot and covered with grayish ash, put the peppers on the grill and cover. Cook for 15 minutes, or until the peppers are soft but still hold their shape.

6 Remove the peppers from the grill and let them cool for a few minutes. Remove the tops, cut the peppers in half, and serve at once.

To serve 4

4 ears of fresh corn

3 tablespoons butter

¾ cup chopped red onion

½ cup sweet green pepper, finely chopped

½ cup tomatoes, chopped

½ teaspoon paprika

Salt and freshly ground black pepper

6 strips of bacon

4 large sweet red peppers

"Only a fool argues with a skunk, a mule, or a cook."
—Ramon F. Adams
Come an' Get It.

ROASTED CORN WITH LIME AND PEQUÍN CHILES

To serve 6

6 ears of fresh corn in the shuck

3 limes

6 pequín chiles

Salt

In Mexico fresh ears of sweet corn are often roasted in braziers over mesquite charcoal and sold to passers-by from corner stands. It is traditional to eat the slightly charred corn rubbed with lime, salt, and fiery pequín chiles.

1 Carefully pull back the husks of the corn without detaching them and remove the corn silk. Pull the husks back into place and tie the ends with a thin strip of the husk.

2 Build a mesquite wood or charcoal fire. When the coals are red-hot and no longer flaming, place the ears of corn deep in the coals. Cover and cook for 20 minutes, turning 2 or 3 times.

3 To serve, pull back 1 strip of the husk to expose the kernels. Quarter the limes and mash the pequín chiles. Serve the corn with individual plates of lime, chiles, and salt.

PATRICIA'S SLIVERED CORN

To make this version of a classic Southern dish, all you need is a dozen very fresh ears of corn, an exceedingly sharp knife, and a large measure of patience. The corn is cut off the cob in tiny slivers and essentially cooks in its own milk. At the end, simply add plenty of sweet butter and a bit of salt and pepper. My grandmother, Patricia Carnal Carr, used to serve this corn on Thanksgiving and Christmas with an oyster-stuffed turkey. It's equally delicious with grilled pork and lamb.

1 Shuck the corn and cut off the stems so that the cobs will stand upright on a cutting board. Using a very sharp paring knife, cut down the cob, removing only the tips of the kernels. Repeat twice, each time slivering a little more off the kernels. Scrape the cob with the knife to remove any remaining pulp.

2 Put the corn and its pulp in a pot and simmer gently over low heat until it is very tender and creamy, about 25 minutes. Remove from the heat, add lots of butter, and sprinkle with salt and pepper to taste. Serve immediately.

To serve 4

12 ears of fresh corn

Sweet butter

Salt and black pepper

NAN'S PAN-FRIED TOMATOES

To serve 4

4 large, ripe tomatoes

½ cup flour

1½ teaspoons sugar

½ teaspoon salt

½ teaspoon freshly ground black pepper

6 tablespoons butter

⅔ cup milk

2 tablespoons sour cream

In August, New Jersey beefsteak tomatoes are at their peak— red, ripe, and full of old-fashioned flavor. It is the perfect time to make this Burlington County farm recipe, which has been in the Black and Newbold families for many generations. Be sure to cook the tomatoes until they are blackened and serve with lots of sour or heavy cream. This dish is very good with grilled meats of all kinds and also tasty on toast.

1 Core the tomatoes and cut them in half. Mix the flour, sugar, salt, and pepper together and lightly dust the tomatoes.

2 Blacken the butter over high heat in a cast-iron skillet. Add the tomatoes, cut side down, and slowly fry them for 8 to 10 minutes, until the cut side has turned very black. Turn the tomatoes over and cook for another 8 to 10 minutes, until the bottoms are blackened and the essence runs out. The tomatoes should be very soft, but still hold their shape.

3 Remove the skillet from the heat and let cool slightly. Stir the milk and sour cream into the pan juices and serve at once.

ACORN SQUASH WITH MAPLE BUTTER

The hard green acorn squash acquires a wonderfully creamy texture when it is baked in the coals of a mesquite fire. Mixed with a bit of butter and maple syrup, it is a delicious accompaniment for grilled rack of lamb or veal chops.

1 Cut each squash in half horizontally. Wrap each half in a double thickness of aluminum foil and close tightly.

2 Build a fire of mesquite wood or charcoal. When the coals are hot, but no longer flaming, nestle the squash in the embers. Cover and cook for 10 minutes. Turn and cook for 10 minutes more, or until the squash is soft but has not lost its shape.

3 Unwrap the squash and carefully scoop out the pulp, reserving the shells. In a bowl, combine the pulp, butter, and maple syrup and blend very well. Return the squash mixture to the shells and serve warm.

To serve 6

3 acorn squash

4 tablespoons butter

2 tablespoons maple syrup

■ FOLK WISDOM

"When the mesquite begins to bud, it's time to put out the tomato plants."

"Plant cotton when the mesquite leafs."

"When the leaves of the mesquite become rusty, rain is not far away."

AURORA'S SUMMER SQUASH WITH HERB BUTTER

To serve 4 to 6

Herb butter:

4 tablespoons sweet
butter, softened

1 tablespoon chives, minced

1 tablespoon fresh basil, minced

1½ teaspoons fresh
marjoram, minced

1½ teaspoons fresh
oregano, minced

1 pound small yellow squash

1 pound small zucchini

1 large yellow onion

2 ears fresh corn

Salt and freshly ground
black pepper

The ingredients in this dish are simplicity itself: yellow crook-neck squash, zucchini, corn, plenty of sweet butter, and herbs. The secret is to use only the freshest, tenderest vegetables and to cook them just until they are soft. This side dish is a fine accompaniment for grilled steaks, lamb chops, pork ribs, and fish.

1 Cream the butter with a fork until it is very soft and smooth. Beat in the herbs and mix well. Set aside in a cool place.

2 Cut the squash and onion in medium dice. Put them in a large pot with ¼ cup water and cover. Cook over medium-low heat until the vegetables are soft and tender, about 15 minutes.

3 Using a potato masher, mash the vegetables thoroughly until they are well mixed. With a sharp knife, cut the kernels off the ears of corn and add them to the squash. Return the mixture to the stove and cook for 6 minutes longer over medium-low heat. Stir in the herb butter, add salt and pepper, and serve at once.

Aurora's Chayote with Tomato and Onion

Chayote, also known as the mirliton or vegetable pear, is a pale green squash that is eaten throughout Latin America, Australia, Indonesia, North Africa, and even in China. As prepared by Aurora Rodriguez, with garlic, onion, and tomato, the chayote is excellent with grilled pork, lamb, or veal.

1 Sauté the chayote in the safflower oil in a large skillet over medium-high heat for 7 to 8 minutes, or until it is barely tender.

2 Add the garlic and onion. Cover, reduce heat to medium, and cook for 5 minutes, or until tender.

3 Add the tomato and cook for another 5 minutes.

4 Remove the chayote from the heat, stir in the cheese, and sprinkle with cilantro.

To serve 4

2 large chayotes, peeled and diced

2 tablespoons safflower oil

3 large cloves garlic, finely chopped

½ cup yellow onion, finely chopped

1 small tomato, peeled, seeded, and chopped

2 tablespoons freshly grated Muenster cheese

1 tablespoon fresh cilantro, minced

FAJITA PARTY
San Ysidro Fajitas with Fresh Tomato Salsa (page 32).
Warm Flour Tortillas.
Chunky Guacamole (page 36).
Aurora's Summer Squash with Herb Butter (page 106).
Flan with Caramelized Sugar.

ROASTED POTATO, BACON, AND SCALLION SALAD

To serve 4

Dressing:

½ cup walnut oil

¼ cup sherry vinegar

1 tablespoon Dijon mustard

1 clove garlic, crushed

Salt and freshly ground
black pepper

2 pounds new potatoes

6 slices thickly cut bacon

¾ cup minced scallions

This twist on a classic potato salad is wonderful when the potatoes and bacon are cooked over a mesquite wood fire. The smoky flavors are enhanced when the salad is served warm with a tangy walnut oil, sherry vinegar, and mustard dressing.

1 Combine the dressing ingredients in a glass bowl and set aside.

2 Scrub and quarter the new potatoes. Wrap them in 5 or 6 packets of double-thickness aluminum foil and seal firmly. Prick the packets with the tines of a fork 3 or 4 times.

3 Put 1 cup of mesquite wood chips in water to soak. Build a fire of mesquite wood. When the coals are red-hot, but no longer flaming, add the wet chips to the coals. Put a cast-iron frying pan on the grill and cover for a few minutes. When the pan is hot, add the slices of bacon. Cover and cook for 2 to 3 minutes per side, or until the bacon is just crisp. Carefully remove the pan, using barbecue mitts or pot holders. Let the bacon drain on a stack of paper towels. Chop finely and set aside.

4 Nestle the potato packets down in the coals and cover. Let them roast for 8 to 10 minutes, then turn and roast for another 8 to 10 minutes. Open 1 packet to make sure the potatoes are cooked through. If not, return them to the coals for a few minutes more.

5 To make the salad, unwrap the potatoes and put them in a large crockery bowl. Add the scallions and salad dressing and toss to coat. Add the chopped bacon and toss again. Serve warm.

HELLZAPOPPIN' POTATO CHIPS

These spicy grilled potato "chips" are a great accompaniment for steaks and chickens cooked over mesquite wood. The fresher and hotter the chili powder is, the tastier the chips will be.

1 Scrub the potatoes well. Put them in a pot of cold water and bring to a boil. Reduce the heat and simmer for 8 to 10 minutes or until the potatoes are barely tender when pricked with a fork.

2 Slice the potatoes into ½-inch slices, leaving the skins on. Brush them generously with olive oil. Peel the garlic clove and cut it in half. Rub the cut sides all over the potato slices. Sprinkle both sides with chili powder and salt to taste.

3 Build a mesquite wood fire. When the coals are red-hot and the flames are low, put the potato slices on the grill and cover. Cook for 4 to 5 minutes per side, or until the potatoes are golden brown and slightly crisp on the outside. (If they start to burn, move them to the edges of the coals.)

To serve 4 to 6

6 large red potatoes

¼ cup extra-virgin olive oil

1 large clove garlic

1 tablespoon chili powder

Salt

MUSHROOMS WITH ROSEMARY AND GARLIC

To serve 4

12 large mushrooms

½ cup extra-virgin olive oil

1 tablespoon minced garlic

1 tablespoon minced fresh rosemary

Salt and freshly ground black pepper

Mushrooms, wild or otherwise, are delicious when brushed with olive oil and sprinkled with a little rosemary and chopped garlic, before being grilled over wood coals. You can use ordinary cultivated or shiitake mushrooms, or if you are very fortunate, you may find fresh porcini ("piglets") imported from Italy during the fall. These nutty-flavored wild mushrooms, some with caps as big as saucers, are a splendid accompaniment to grilled steaks.

1 Remove the stems and reserve for another use. Wipe the caps clean with a damp cloth.

2 Combine the olive oil, garlic, and rosemary in a small bowl. Brush the mixture over the mushrooms and set aside.

3 Build a fire of ⅓ mesquite wood and ⅔ mesquite charcoal. When the coals are medium-hot and covered with gray ash, put the mushrooms on the grill and cover. Cook for 3 to 4 minutes per side, or until cooked through.

4 Remove the mushrooms from the grill, sprinkle with a little salt and pepper, and serve at once.

WILD MUSHROOM SCRAMBLE

The earthy flavor of wild mushrooms sautéed with herbs complements the taste of duck or other game birds grilled over mesquite. You can use almost any combination of wild mushrooms, but this dish is most delectable when they are fresh.

1 Remove the stems from the mushrooms and reserve for another use. Wipe the caps with a damp cloth. Slice thin.

2 In a large skillet, melt 1 tablespoon of butter over medium-high heat. Add the shallots and sauté for 3 minutes.

3 Reduce the heat to medium and add the rest of the butter, mushrooms, herbs, salt, and pepper. Cook for 3 to 4 minutes, stirring constantly.

4 Reduce the heat to low, cover, and cook very slowly for 15 minutes. Taste and correct the seasonings if necessary.

To serve 4

¼ pound fresh morels

¼ pound fresh shiitake mushrooms

¼ pound fresh golden oak mushrooms

4 tablespoons sweet butter

½ cup shallots, thinly sliced

1 teaspoon fresh rosemary, minced

1 teaspoon fresh tarragon, minced

1 teaspoon fresh thyme, minced

**To serve 6 as a main course
or 12 as a side dish**

2 pounds pinto beans

½ pound ham, coarsely chopped

1 large yellow onion, finely chopped

1 scallion, finely chopped

1 bunch cilantro, finely chopped

1 canned jalapeño pepper
plus 1 teaspoon of the pickling juice

1 large clove garlic, finely chopped

1 small tomato, finely chopped

Salt

One of the most delicious ways of cooking pinto beans, or frijoles, is to simmer them in a heavy pot over a mesquite fire. The firm but tender beans, swimming in a rich, smoky broth flavored with ham and cilantro and spiked with a fiery jalapeño pepper, make a fine accompaniment for grilled beef or pork. They can also make a splendid supper dish in themselves, served with warm tortillas, a tossed green salad, and plenty of ice-cold beer.

Be sure to use a heavy-bottomed pot that can stand up to the heat of a mesquite fire. If the pot is too large to fit under the cover of your grill, you can create a makeshift cover of heavy-duty aluminum foil to capture both the heat and aroma of the fire.

1 Wash the beans carefully and pick out grit and empty hulls. Put the beans in a large bowl, cover with cold water, and soak

Continued on next page

MESQUITE-SMOKED PINTO BEANS

for 3 hours or overnight. Drain the water. Put the beans in a large heavy-bottomed pot and add 12 cups of cold water.

2 Put 3 cups of mesquite wood chips in water to soak. Build a fire of mesquite charcoal. As soon as the coals are well lit and the flames are just licking the bottom of the grill, put a cup of wet chips on the fire. Place the pot of beans on the grill and cover. Simmer for approximately 2 hours, until the beans are tender but still firm—do not let them get mushy. Add water if all the liquid is absorbed before the beans are done. Every 30 minutes or so, check the fire and add fresh charcoal and a few wet chips to the coals if necessary.

3 After 2 hours, add the ham to the pot and simmer for 10 minutes. Add the onions, cilantro, jalapeño pepper and its liquid, and garlic, and simmer for another 10 minutes. Remove the beans from the heat. Stir in the tomato and add salt to taste. Serve the beans in pottery bowls with warm tortillas on the side.

■ *SUNDAY RANCH BRUNCH*

Pork and Venison Sausage with Cilantro (page 62).

Eggs Scrambled with Diced Cactus Leaf.

Tart Tomatillo Sauce (page 118).

Mesquite-Smoked Pinto Beans (page 112).

Homemade Biscuits.

Mesquite Bean Jelly (page 125).

Catarina Pear Apple Jelly (page 126).

Cafe con Piquete (Coffee Spiked with Tequila).

CARMEN'S BEST RICE

To serve 4 to 6

1 cup white rice

1 tablespoon plus
1 teaspoon extra-virgin olive oil

½ cup onion, diced small

2 large garlic cloves, minced

½ cup tomato, finely chopped

½ cup potatoes, peeled
and diced small

¼ cup fresh peas

1 tablespoon carrots, minced

1 chicken thigh

2 cups water

1 teaspoon salt

1 tablespoon fresh cilantro, minced

Freshly ground black pepper

The secret of Carmen Ramos' superb rice is a leisurely sautéing in oil until it is golden and the addition of tiny bits of vegetables. It is further enriched with a small piece of chicken and left to simmer until it is fluffy. Serve the rice with grilled fish or wild game.

1 In a large skillet, sauté the rice in the olive oil over medium-high heat until it begins to turn golden.

2 Add the onions and garlic and sauté for 2 minutes, or until they soften, stirring constantly. Reduce the heat to medium.

3 Add the tomatoes and cook for 2 minutes, continuing to stir.

4 Add the potatoes, carrots, and peas and cook for 2 minutes, stirring constantly.

5 Add the chicken thigh and cook for 3 to 4 minutes, or until the skin is lightly browned.

6 Add the water and salt. Bring to a boil, cover, and reduce heat to low. Simmer for 15 to 20 minutes, or until the water is completely absorbed and the rice is fluffy. Stir in the cilantro and add pepper to taste.

SALSAS, SAUCES, JELLIES, AND BREADS

FRESH TOMATO SALSA

Makes 3½ cups

1 pound ripe tomatoes

1 medium yellow onion

2 cloves garlic

1 bunch cilantro

2 fresh serrano chiles

Juice of 1 lime

Salt

This classic salsa picante, also known as pico de gallo, is the perfect accompaniment for fajitas, grilled chicken, and even scrambled eggs. For best results, make it at least an hour ahead of time so that the flavors can mingle.

1 Finely chop the tomatoes. Peel and finely chop the onion. Peel and mince the garlic. Remove the stems of the cilantro and mince the leaves. Remove the stems and seeds of the serrano chiles and mince.

2 Combine all the ingredients in a large bowl. Set aside for 30 minutes. Taste and correct seasonings. The salsa is best served fresh but will keep for 2 days in the refrigerator.

LUCY'S PIQUE

Lucy Sepulveda first prepared this fresh Colombian-style salsa to go with empanadas, but it is equally delicious with grilled chicken and fish. It's called "pique" because of the "bite" or "sting" of the fiery little pequín chiles.

■ In a glass bowl, combine the tomato, onion, cilantro, water, lemon juice, and oil. Mash the pequín chiles with a fork, or in a mortar and pestle, and stir into the salsa. Add salt to taste.

■ Refrigerate the salsa for 1 hour; then taste and correct seasonings. (If it is too hot for your liking, drain the liquid and add fresh water and lemon juice.) The pique will keep for 2 days in the refrigerator.

Makes 1 cup

1 firm, ripe tomato, finely chopped

¼ cup green scallion tops, finely chopped

1 small bunch cilantro, finely chopped

¼ cup water

3 tablespoons lemon juice

1 teaspoon extra-virgin olive oil

3 to 4 pequín chiles, or to taste

Salt

■ *"Woe to the cook whose sauce has no sting."*
—*Chaucer*

TART TOMATILLO SAUCE

Makes 3 cups

2 pounds tomatillos

1 tablespoon cumin seeds

8 cloves garlic

1 or 2 serrano chiles, stems and seeds removed, chopped

1 medium onion, chopped

1 bunch cilantro, chopped

This tasty salsa is made from the tiny green tomatoes known as tomatillos or fresadillas. In the markets you'll find them in their papery husks—even the ripe ones are yellowish-green and their flesh is firmer and crisper than that of their big red relatives. The sauce is delicious with simply grilled cabrito, chicken, and pork. It's also excellent with scrambled eggs.

1 Remove the husks from the tomatillos. Wash them well, remove the cores, and cut in half. Put them in a nonaluminum pot with 2 tablespoons of water. Add the cumin, garlic, and serrano chiles and cook over medium heat for about 40 minutes, or until the tomatillos become very soft.

2 Purée the tomatillo mixture in a blender or food processor for 15 seconds. (Or mash them with a potato masher.) Return them to the pot and add the onions and cilantro. Cook over medium heat for 15 minutes. Add salt to taste.

3 Let the tomatillo sauce cool to room temperature before pouring it into a large glass jar. The sauce will keep in the refrigerator for 3 or 4 days.

MESQUITE BARBECUE SAUCE, SMOKY NO. 1

This is a sweet-sour-hot sauce with dark, smoky undertones. Flavored with orange zest, fresh ginger, and fiery serrano peppers, the sauce gets an added boost from a dash of liquid mesquite smoke, a natural product derived from condensed wood smoke. Because of the citrus flavoring, this sauce is especially good with pork and duck.

1 Combine the tomato purée, onion, ginger, garlic, orange zest, and serrano chiles in a nonaluminum saucepan. Simmer over low heat for 1½ hours, until reduced to approximately 2 cups.

2 Put the tomato mixture in a blender or food processor and purée until very smooth. Strain through a sieve or strainer, pressing on the solids with the back of a wooden spoon.

3 Put the tomato mixture in a clean nonaluminum saucepan. Add the rest of the ingredients and simmer over low heat for 10 minutes. Let cool and pour into a jar. The sauce will keep for 1 week in the refrigerator.

Makes about 1½ cups

4 cups fresh tomato purée

1½ cups chopped onion

2 tablespoons fresh ginger, peeled and chopped

1 tablespoon chopped garlic

2 tablespoons slivered orange zest

2 serrano chiles, seeded and cut into strips

½ cup honey

¼ cup lemon juice

2 tablespoons soy sauce

1 tablespoon Worcestershire sauce

1 tablespoon vinegar

¾ teaspoon liquid mesquite smoke

Salt and freshly ground black pepper

"[Grandaddy] tol' us, 'Don' ever give nobody your barbecue recipe because then they don' need you. Long as a man don' know what you know, ain't nothin' he can be but nice."
—Thomas Jackson, Atlanta barbecue cook

TEXAS HOT PEPPER SAUCE

Makes 1 cup

1 cup white wine vinegar

4 tablespoons pequín chiles

1 sprig fresh thyme

½ teaspoon salt

This traditional hot sauce is a great way to perk up plain grilled pork and chicken. Some even like it on their steaks. Old recipes call for mixing equal quantities of vinegar and pequín chiles, a ferocious brew that will blister the skin right off your tongue. This newer version is plenty hot as it is and should be used sparingly.

1 Combine all the ingredients in a glass jar and close tightly. Let the mixture steep for 1 week, shaking it several times a day. At the end of a week, strain and pour into a shaker bottle. The hot sauce will keep indefinitely.

DOWN-EAST MOPPIN' AND SOPPIN' SAUCE

Goldsboro is a little town near the North Carolina coast that is famed for its extraordinarily good pork barbecue. Whole hogs are slowly cooked over hardwood coals until the meat is so tender it nearly falls off the bone. The rich pork—fat, skin, and all—is then chopped up and served with liberal dousings of this hot vinegar sauce. The sauce is an excellent accompaniment for any grilled pork or chicken.

1 Combine all the ingredients in a bowl and mix well. Pour into a shaker bottle. Keeps indefinitely.

Makes 1 cup

1 cup cider vinegar

2 teaspoons ground red pepper

1 teaspoon ground black pepper

½ teaspoon salt

1 teaspoon safflower oil

MESQUITE ETIQUETTE
Letitia Baldrige, America's arbiter of manners, has these tips for barbecue etiquette:

For hosts: "Provide lots of oversized paper napkins, 3 or 4 per guest. Be sure that sauce is served in clean, nongreasy containers. After the meal, finger bowls are a splendid touch—use bowls filled with warm water and floating slices of lemon."

For guests: "Just because a barbecue is an informal affair, don't think you don't have to write a thank-you note. A cookout is a lot of trouble to put on, and your hosts will appreciate the extra effort of a thank-you note."

QUICK FOUR PEPPER RELISH

Makes 1 cup

1 pound tomatoes, peeled,
seeded, and chopped

1 cup red onion, finely chopped

½ cup sweet green pepper, chopped

½ cup sweet red pepper, chopped

½ cup sweet yellow pepper, chopped

1 or 2 fresh serrano peppers,
seeded and minced

2 tablespoons white wine vinegar

1 tablespoon brown sugar

This peppery relish is sweet and hot at the same time. Try it with plain grilled hamburgers, chicken, and lamb chops.

1 Combine all the ingredients in a nonaluminum saucepan and simmer gently for 40 minutes, stirring frequently. Add a little water if the mixture begins to stick.

2 Cool to room temperature and pour into a glass jar. The relish can be kept refrigerated for 1 week.

OMAMA'S RELISH

This is my grandmother Emma Neuen Beinhorn's recipe for tomato, onion, pepper, and cabbage relish. Making it used to be a wearying labor of love, since all the vegetables had to be finely chopped by hand. Today you can still chop them by hand, or you can use a food processor. Either way, this is a superb relish that is excellent with barbecued brisket or any other grilled meat.

I've cut the original recipe in half, but it is so good that you may want to double the recipe the second time around and make the full 12 pints.

1 Using a sharp knife or a food processor, finely chop the vegetables. If you use the food processor, chop each vegetable separately by pulsing the machine on and off. Do not let the vegetables get mushy. Combine the vegetables in 1 or more large bowls and add the salt. Let stand for 3 hours. Drain thoroughly through a layer of cheesecloth.

2 In a large nonaluminum pot, combine the rest of the ingredients and bring to a boil. Boil for 2 minutes. Add the chopped vegetables, bring to a boil, and cook for 5 minutes. Seal hot in hot sterilized jars.

Makes 6 pints

2½ pounds green unripe tomatoes

2½ pounds red ripe tomatoes

3 fresh jalapeño peppers

1 small head cabbage, about 2 pounds

6 medium green bell peppers

6 medium onions

6 tablespoons salt

1½ pounds sugar

1 tablespoon ginger

1 tablespoon dry mustard

1½ teaspoons turmeric

1½ teaspoons celery seed

½ teaspoon cloves

½ teaspoon ground cinnamon

1 quart apple cider vinegar

A SAVORY BEAN
What do mesquite beans really taste like? Peter Felker, a research scientist at Texas A&I University in Kingsville—and a man with an abiding passion for the mesquite tree—compares the juicy unripe pods to snow peas or bing cherries. The mature, dry beans, on the other hand, have the flavor of molasses or burnt coffee—which may be the reason why, during the Civil War when real coffee could not be had, a lot of folks drank a brew made of ground-up mesquite beans.

PAT'S LOUISIANA PEACH CHUTNEY

Makes 5-6 pints

3½ pounds fresh peaches, peeled and cut into medium-sized pieces

5 cooking apples, peeled and cut small

2 cups onions, chopped

4 pounds cane sugar

1½ pints vinegar

3 or 4 hot red peppers, seeds removed

1 cup sultana raisins

1 cup dried currants

2 teaspoons cinammon

1 teaspoon ginger

1 teaspoon salt

1 teaspoon allspice

½ teaspoon cloves

This is a wonderful, old-time Louisiana recipe for peach chutney that Pat Dunk used to make every summer when the peaches ripened on the trees in her California garden. Her daughter Victoria remembers that the chutney was cooked in an enormous pot and that it took all day to prepare it, since Pat usually doubled the recipe. The chutney is delicious with lamb, pork, duck, and chicken, and it's also just fine eaten right out of the jar.

1 Boil the vinegar and sugar for 15 minutes.

2 Skim and add peaches and apples. Lower the heat and simmer 10 minutes.

3 Add onions and peppers. Cook 15 minutes, stirring often.

4 Add currants and raisins. Cook 10 minutes.

5 Add spices and salt. Cook 30 minutes.

6 Seal in sterile jars.

MESQUITE BEAN JELLY

When the summers are hot and dry, the mesquite tree produces magnificent crop of sweet, succulent beans. This is the time to pick the beans from the trees and use them to make a pale gold, delicately flavored jelly that is excellent with grilled meats and also very tasty with breakfast biscuits.

To be sure you're getting the best beans, walk around and taste pods from different trees until you find some that are very sweet and juicy. Avoid those with bug holes in them, and don't use any that have fallen to the ground.

This recipe is based on one from the Institute of Texan Cultures in San Antonio.

■ Wash the beans, break them into pieces, and put them in a large pot with 8 cups of water to cover. Bring to a boil. Boil for 15 to 20 minutes. Let the juice cool. Strain through a clean cloth. There should be 4 cups.

■ Put the 4 cups of juice in a clean pot. Add 1 package Sure-Jell and bring to a boil. Boil for 1 minute. Add 4 cups of sugar. Bring to a boil. Boil 1 minute. Pour into hot sterilized jars and seal while hot.

Makes 2½ pints

1 large handful mesquite beans

4 cups sugar

1 package Sure-Jell

■ *THE FALSE PEACH*
Many an early Texas traveler mistook the mesquite tree, with its short trunk and deeply forked branches, for a peach. But it was poet Sidney Lanier who was inspired to describe the similarity most lyrically. In 1872, after journeying in the New Braunfels area at night, he wrote: "Presently I observed the stage lamps continually light up a curious sort of bare struggling-twigged shrub that seems to line the road and cover the prairie. It is as if the apparitions of all the lifeless peach orchards in Georgia were lawlessly dancing past us."

Makes 11 to 12 pints

1 gallon red ripe prickly pears (pick them with kitchen tongs)

2½ packages Sure-Jell (5 tablespoons to a package)

½ cup lemon juice

9 cups sugar

In the thorniest part of the brush country, nopal cactus is nearly as ubiquitous as the mesquite. In the summer the nopal produces a delicious fruit—the reddish-purple, thorn-studded pear apple, or prickly pear. It is wonderful eaten right off the cactus (once you've gotten past those hair-like thorns) or when made into a rosy-colored jelly. Pear apple jelly is very tasty with mesquite-grilled sausage or as an accompaniment for any sort of wild game.

This recipe comes from *The Catarina Cookbook,* a colorful compendium of brush country recipes.

1 Singe the thorns off the prickly pears by holding them in the flame of a gas burner or a candle. Wash off the burn marks and put the prickly pears in a large nonaluminum pot with water to cover. Boil until tender, but do not mash. Pour off the juice. There should be 6 cups.

2 In a large nonaluminum pot, combine the pear apple juice, lemon juice, and Sure-Jell. Add the sugar and boil 3 minutes. Remove from the heat immediately. Seal hot in hot sterilized jars.

MIMI'S BUTTERMILK CORNBREAD WITH GREEN CHILES

My mother Phyllis Beinhorn's old-fashioned cornbread has a wonderful custard-like texture and rich buttery flavor. The green chiles add just a hint of fire. This cornbread is especially good with grilled wild hog or any other pork cooked over mesquite wood.

■ Roast the poblano chiles in an open flame or under the oven broiler until the skin is blackened and blistered all over. Put the chiles in a plastic sack or paper bag, close tightly, and let them steam for 10 minutes. Remove them from the bag and rub off the skin with your fingers. Remove the stems and seeds and cut the chiles into ¼-inch dice.

■ Preheat the oven to 375°F.

■ Combine the cornmeal, baking soda, and salt in a large glass bowl and mix well. Beat the eggs until they are frothy and slowly add them to the dry ingredients. Gradually pour in the buttermilk and stir to mix well. Add the melted butter and mix well. Add the diced chiles and stir to distribute them throughout the batter.

■ Put a 9- by 12-inch glass baking dish into the oven to warm it slightly. Remove and rub the inside with safflower oil. Pour the cornbread batter into the dish and place it on the middle rack of the oven. Bake for 20 to 25 minutes, or until the center is firm and the edges have begun to pull away from the sides of the pan.

■ Let the cornbread cool slightly. Cut it into squares and serve with plenty of sweet butter.

To serve 6

2 poblano chiles

1½ cups fresh stone-ground cornmeal

1 teaspoon baking soda

1 teaspoon salt

2 cups buttermilk at room temperature

2 eggs at room temperature

2 tablespoons melted butter

1 tablespoon safflower oil

■ *WORDS TO EAT BY*
"A lean belly never feeds a fat brain."
—*Ramon F. Adams,*
Come an' Get It.

LUCY'S CORNCAKES

To make 8 arepas

2 cups precooked cornmeal for arepas (sold in Latin American markets)

1 teaspoon salt

1 cup freshly grated mild white cheddar cheese

½ tablespoon butter

These tasty cornmeal cakes are known as arepas in Colombia and other Latin American countries. Traditionally, arepas are patted and turned in a complicated series of hand maneuvers until they resemble small wheels with a rim and a hub. This simpler version is patted or rolled with a pin, and tastes just as good. Serve arepas with a whole suckling pig or any grilled pork dish. They are also delicious served with thinly sliced mesquite-grilled steak.

1 Combine the cornmeal, salt, cheese and butter. Add 1¼ cups of lukewarm water and knead the ingredients for 3 minutes. The dough should be soft and smooth, but not sticky. If it is too dry, add a little more water. Roll the dough into a ball and set it aside for 15 minutes.

2 To make the arepas, pinch off about ⅛ of the dough. Roll it between the palms of your hands until it forms a slightly flattened sphere. Place it on a flat surface and pat or roll the dough into a disk about ½ inch thick. Pick it up and rub your finger around the edges to smooth them. Repeat with the rest of the dough.

3 To cook, coat the bottom of cast-iron frying pan with 1 teaspoon of corn oil. Heat the pan over medium-low heat and add the arepas. Cook them very slowly until they are slightly browned on both sides. Or, cook the arepas on the grill over medium-hot coals for 4 minutes per side. Serve while still warm.

DESSERT IDEAS

What's a fitting finish to a mesquite-grilled dinner? Light desserts using lots of fresh fruit, says Lindsey Shere, author of *Chez Panisse Desserts,* who's been turning out delectable mousses, tarts and other goodies for Chez Panisse for 15 years. Here are a few of Lindsey's suggestions:

1. Passion fruit mousse with lightly sugared, sliced strawberries.

2. Peach crisp or cobbler with vanilla ice cream.

3. Cooling citrus-flavored sherbets: grapefruit, blood orange or tangerine, lemon or Meyer lemon (a lemon-orange cross).

4. Cream puffs filled with strawberry ice cream and fresh strawberries.

5. Cold mango or papaya, sprinkled with rum, lime juice, and grated lime peel.

6. Orange-pineapple or blood orange upside-down cake.

7. Ambrosia: layers of oranges, blood oranges, and coconut.

8. Lime mousse sprinkled with grated lime peel.

9. Fresh peach or blackberry short cake.

10. Ripe bananas halved lengthwise, sprinkled with rum and brown sugar, dotted with butter and baked in foil on the grill.

11. Fruit soups of puréed blackberries and strawberries with sugar and kirsch to taste, served in soup plates and garnished with thinly sliced fruit such as star fruit, pineapple, blood orange, kiwi, melon, plums, peaches, nectarines or passion fruit pulp.

12. Apples cored and stuffed with brown sugar, butter, cinnamon, raisins and walnuts, baked in foil on the grill and served with thick cream.

13. Fresh peach ice cream.

14. Poached peaches with bourbon-flavored sabayon.

GOOD READING

The following books and articles are recommended for further reading about mesquite—its botany, folklore, and culinary uses:

Beinhorn, Courtenay. "Mesquite: Bad Press but Great Flavor," *The New York Times.* June 23, 1982.

Beinhorn, Courtenay. "The Mesquite Mystique," *Ultra.* August 1983.

Dobie, J. Frank. "Mesquite," *The Southwestern Sheep & Goat Raiser.* December 1, 1938.

Dobie, J. Frank. "Mesquite," *Arizona Highways.* November 1941. [Essentially the same article as above.]

Felker, Peter, and Robertson, Sheila. *Mesquite Woodworking.* Kingsville, Texas: Caesar Kleberg Wildlife Research Institute, 1983.

Peattie, Donald Culross. *A Natural History of Western Trees.* Boston: Houghton Mifflin, 1953.

Weiner, Michael A. *Earth Medicine, Earth Food.* New York: Macmillan, 1980.

Wilson, Steve. "Mesquite: Wonder Tree of the Southwest," *Texas Highways.* July, 1979.

Wright, Carl C. "The Mesquite Tree: From Nature's Boon to Aggressive Invader," *Southwestern Historical Quarterly,* Vol. 69.

The Mesquite Messenger. Austin, Texas: Los Amigos Del Mesquite. [Published quarterly since 1984.]

"Smoke-barbecuing Secrets," *Sunset Magazine.* August 1983.

The following books are excellent sources of information about outdoor cookery and were helpful in the preparation of this book.

Adams, Ramon F. *Come an' Get It, The Story of the Old Cowboy Cook.* Norman: University of Oklahoma Press, 1952. [Amusing reminiscences and lingo of old time trail chefs.]

Brown, Helen Evans, and Beard, James A. *The Complete Book of Outdoor Cookery.* Garden City, New York: Doubleday, 1955. [Solid grilling information. Hundreds of recipes, although a little dated.]

Coleman, Arthur and Bobbie. *The Texas Cookbook, Culinary and Campfire Lore from the Lone Star State.* New York: A. A. Wyn, 1949. [Still the best Texas cookbook. A treasure trove of traditional recipes. Witty and informative.]

David, Elizabeth. *Elizabeth David Classics.* New York: Alfred A. Knopf, 1980. [A single volume containing three of this English food writer's best known books—*A Book of Mediterranean Food, French Country Cooking,* and *Summer Cooking,* all of which have recipes to inspire the outdoor chef.]

Sinnes, A. Cort. *The Grilling Book.* Berkeley and Los Angeles: Aris Books, 1985. [An excellent primer of grilling techniques. Recipes by Jay Harlow, a professional grill chef.]

Waldron, Maggie. *Barbecue & Smoke Cookery.* San Francisco: 101 Productions, 1983. [An international collection of barbecue recipes, with good information on smoke cooking.]

Waters, Alice. *The Chez Panisse Menu Cookbook.* New York: Random House, 1982. [Imaginative, innovative recipes from the West Coast restaurant that did much to popularize the mesquite grill.]

Outdoor Cooking, from *The Good Cook/Techniques & Recipes* series. Alexandria, Virginia: Time-Life Books, 1983. [Richard Olney and Jeremiah Tower consulted on this superb book. Excellent information on outdoor cooking techniques, with helpful color photographs and many imaginative recipes.]

■ *Courtenay Beinhorn grew up cooking with mesquite wood on the San Ysidro Ranch in south Texas. She writes about food and entertaining for the* New York Times, Ultra, Savvy, *and many other publications. She now resides in New York with her husband and daughter.*